TURNING → POINTS

TURNING → POINTS

Charles Sharpe
An Autobiography

Foreword by Senator John Ashcroft

Note: Most of the Scripture quotations in this book are from the New
International Version.

Cover photography by Jim Whitmer, Chicago, Illinois.
Cover design by John Gilmore, Houston, Texas.
Edited by Stan Campbell, Woodridge, Illinois.
Layout design by Catherine Springle, Friendswood, Texas.

To Laurie, my true love and my partner
in everything we do.

ACKNOWLEDGMENTS

As I look back on my life, I am always struck by the fact that several Ozark National Life executives stood by me when I needed them most. To honor them, I have interviewed many of them for this book. They are business associates, but much more, they are dear friends: Hugh Wyatt, Tom Brandt, Richard Luelf, Gene Montee, and Al Weber.

Long-time Ozark employees have shared my ups and downs. They have seen me at my worst, yet they chose to hang in there with me. I deeply appreciate their loyalty. A few of them were interviewed for this book: Harry Stauffer, Linda Gensler, Dianna Cardello, and Lorrie Lasater.

I cherish the relationship I have with my children, Rodney, Linda, and Carol. God restored our relationship and gave us a genuine love for each other.

Jon Simmons has been the General Manager of Sharpe Land & Cattle, our farming, cattle, and dairy operation in northeast Missouri, for 19 years. John's hard work is matched by his wisdom in the day-to-day decisions that have to be made in running such a large business like this. He is a real partner—more like a son to me.

The people who have helped build Heartland are also very special to me. They have come because they want to pour out their lives to serve God in helping people. Scores could have been included in these pages, but we interviewed only a couple of them. I want to thank Taysir S. Abu Saada (Tass) for his testimony in this book. My grandson, Rob Patchin, represents the heart and soul of our ministry to young people. God gave Rob a love for troubled young men, and he became the director of our Recovery Center. Under his able leadership, these young men receive godly instruction, accountability, and the love of Christ.

My secretary, Rhonda Morgan, helps me in so many ways. Her tireless work is matched by her cheerful attitude. She has coordinated many of the logistics so this book could be completed.

This book probably wouldn't have been written if Al Denson hadn't pushed a little bit. Al's music and his friendship mean so much to me and to the people at Heartland and Ozark.

And finally, I want to thank Pat Springle for helping me shape my story so it communicates my heart.

TABLE OF CONTENTS

Foreword 11

Introduction 15

1 Not Far From the Tree 19

2 A Few Good Men 37

3 Foundations 53

4 Betrayal 89

5 Rock Bottom . . . and Rebound 103

6 A New Love 149

7 The Prodigal Returns 163

8 Heartland 201

9 Laurie's Story 267

10 Looking Back . . . Looking Forward 293

Epilogue 333

John Ashcroft
United States Senator

FOREWORD

Passionate . . . warm . . . action-oriented . . . forthright
. . . enthusiastic . . . unpretentious. These are words that
come to mind when I think of my friend Charlie Sharpe.

Charlie and I met more than 25 years ago, when Charlie
was building his business, Ozark National Life Insurance
Company. My brother Bob was one of his employees. Bob
introduced us, and it became obvious very quickly that
Charlie and I held similar beliefs and shared a vision for
Missouri and our country.

In 1984, when I ran for Governor of Missouri, Charlie
was someone who supported my goals for the state. Our
relationship expanded beyond politics, and I am fortunate
to view Charlie Sharpe as a good friend. He has been very
kind to me throughout my public service in Jefferson City
and, since 1994, in the United States Senate. I greatly value
his insights and ideas for calling our country to her highest
and best.

Charlie Sharpe is a gracious person. But he is also a man of action. He knows how to motivate people to give all they've got in order to accomplish big things. One of my favorite memories is when Charlie asked me to speak at a dinner for his company's policyholders. Charlie jumped on stage to give me a rousing introduction. He said that America needs leaders with sound principles and the courage to act on them. It was one of the most stirring and compelling introductions I've ever heard. I was deeply grateful for his words. My hope is that I can live up to a small part of Charlie's expectations. Charlie Sharpe has that effect on people — he motivates to reach above themselves.

Charlie is right about the need for leadership in America. Some people think that "leadership" is like driving a taxi: You ask people where they want to go and offer to drive them there. But that's not leadership. Those who are entrusted with the responsibility of leadership should call people to their highest and best, not encourage us to perform at our lowest and least. Charlie Sharpe doesn't need a public opinion poll to know right from wrong. His faith in God and his conscience determine that for him. His passion is to motivate people to live by eternally valid values of honor, responsibility, and goodness.

Values are taught through meaningful relationships. Our relationships with our Creator, and with other people, enable us to focus our lives on love, truth, and integrity. As these relationships flourish, the guides of faith, family, and freedom provide meaning and stability to our lives. Charlie would tell you — does tell you, in this book — about how relationships have been at the center of what he has been able to achieve.

In recent years, Charlie has focused his time and talent on creating Heartland, a community in northeastern Missouri where life's most important foundational values can be taught to young people who need a pilot through storms in their lives. Throughout his life, Charlie has had an incredible capacity to focus his energy and resources on specific goals. Now his drive is to see God work deeply and profoundly to change lives. One marker of his passion for ministry is that he gets up each morning at about 4:30, so he can devote the first hours of each day to prayer. He is a powerful and productive man. But he realizes that all he has belongs to the Lord, and he knows that only the Lord has the power to transform lives for the good.

I am delighted that Charlie has responded to those who have asked him to write a book about his life. It is a pleasure and a blessing to be able to recommend his values and life to the attention of others. I feel certain that those who read the Charlie Sharpe story will come to cherish the man, his message, and his mission.

John Ashcroft
United States Senator
May 1999

INTRODUCTION

God is always at work. Sometimes His hand on our lives is very obvious; sometimes it remains a mystery for years. In either case, we can be very sure that God is active. His loving hand is shaping our lives even when we don't recognize it at all.

This book is the story of how God has been at work in my life since I was a little boy. As I have traveled around the country to speak about how God has been faithful in every detail of my life, many people have told me, "Charlie, you need to write a book about all this!" Up to now, I've avoided writing my story. I started a time or two, but the timing just didn't seem right. At this point in my life, however, God has given me a green light. My story demonstrates the incredible mercy and goodness of God to someone who at first wasn't very responsive to Him. And it is the story of how God can use people—even those with foibles and faults as big as mine—if we are willing to put ourselves in His strong and gracious hands.

This is not primarily the story of Ozark National Life, but rather the account of how God provided the wisdom to create that company. More than a story of difficult business and personal circumstances, this is a description of how God engineered those circumstances to teach His lessons and work His will. To some extent it is the story of an older man finding something to occupy his time, but even more so it is the chronicle of God's clear direction to create Heartland, a Christian community devoted to truth and healing.

> **God has sometimes seemed like He was a million miles away and without the slightest inclination to care about my life. But even then, He was at work.**

Not everything in these pages is positive and pleasant. To explain the grace of God, I must describe how desperately I have needed His grace. To demonstrate the power of God, I need to tell about my many failures. God has sometimes seemed like He was a million miles away and without the slightest inclination to care about my life. But even then, He was at work.

A passage of Scripture that has meant a lot to me comes from the Book of Isaiah where the prophet quotes God. The people were facing difficult circumstances, and were confused. The more they tried to figure things out, the more baffled they became. The Lord wanted to convince them that He had not stopped caring or working in their lives. Even in their discouragement, God provided strong assurance of His gracious purposes toward them:

"For my thoughts are not your thoughts,
neither are your ways my ways," declares the Lord.
"As the heavens are higher than the earth,
so are my ways higher than your ways
and my thoughts than your thoughts.
As the rain and the snow come down from heaven,
and do not return to it without watering the earth
and making it bud and flourish, so that it yields seed for
the sower and bread for the eater,
so is my word that goes out from my mouth;
It will not return to me empty,
but will accomplish what I desire and achieve the
purpose for which I sent it." (Isaiah 55:8-11)

This book is my story of God's thoughts and God's ways with me. They are always far higher—and far better—than anything I could possibly imagine. As I grow in my relationship with Christ, I am more in tune with His purposes, and I sense His direction more and more. But even when I don't know what He is doing, I can be sure His plan is good, loving, and wise. I am convinced because I have seen Him at work so many times throughout the course of my life. I hope this story encourages you, too, to trust His hand and His heart in your life.

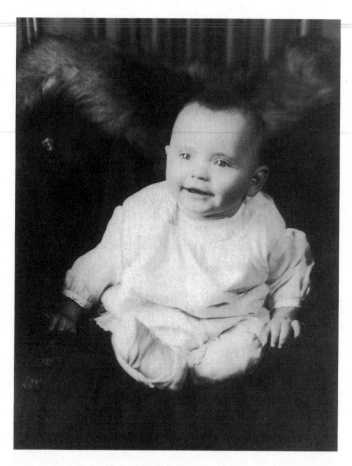

About seven months old

CHAPTER 1

NOT FAR FROM THE TREE

They say an apple doesn't fall far from the tree. That is certainly true of me and my father.

I was born in 1927 into a family of farmers in Lewis County, Missouri. I became a teenager during the years of the Great Depression in the 1930s. Those were tough, tough times. A common misconception about those years is that farmers could withstand anything because they grew their own food. But farmers also had to pay taxes on their land, buy clothes for their families, and maintain tools to keep their farms productive. Some areas of the United States had 40 percent unemployment, so people didn't have enough money to afford food grown on the farms. During this period, the government paid farmers to get rid of their hogs—to shoot them and bury them—because the price of hogs was so low that farmers couldn't afford to feed them. The Depression robbed farmers and their families of their source of livelihood . . . and of their dignity. Those who survived became strong. I grew up during this time when you had to work hard and make great sacrifices just to hang on to your land.

I was the youngest of four children. My brother Wilbur was eleven years older, and there were two sisters between Wilbur and me. I had the greatest parents, Norval and Lois, any child could ask for. They were wonderful people who weren't Christians, but were better role models than many Christians I know. I loved my sisters, but they irritated me a lot. They often whined about me, "Mom, can't you make him be quiet?" I guess I talked a lot, and I was incredibly active. (Today, doctors would take one look at me and immediately write a prescription for Ritalin or Prozak.) My mother never let me go too far. She would "get on my case" if I got out of line. She would say, "Look! I'm telling you, Charlie, cool it!" If I didn't respond, she got the razor strap. That always got my attention! She didn't *threaten* to use it. She just used it!

My dad whipped me only once in my life. I was very small—around three or four years old, but I remember that moment very well! I hid from him in a post pile. He looked all over the farm, but he couldn't find me. I thought it was great fun. Obviously he didn't! After a while, he began to worry because he thought I might be lost or badly hurt. He'd been looking for a long time when he came to the post pile. He called my name as I looked out through the posts at him. When he finally found me, he was really excited . . . and really mad!

There wasn't a prolonged trial. Dad was the prosecutor, judge, jury, and executioner all in one! Right there, right then—I experienced instant judgment on my rear end as he blistered my bottom! The spanking really didn't hurt that much, but it hurt my feelings. I still remember it like it was yesterday. At that moment, I made up my mind that I was not going to do anything to let that happen again. I wanted to please my father, and I knew I had let him down.

My dad had no tolerance for delayed obedience. When he gave an order, he expected it to be carried out at once. He would say, "Son, I want you to go get me a hammer," and what he meant was, "I don't want to be a lot older than I am now when you get back with it." That's the way it was. I've often said that I didn't walk until I was fifteen because I *ran* all the time. My dad was always in a hurry. I

> I made up my mind that I was not going to do anything to let that happen again. I wanted to please my father, and I knew I had let him down.

loved being with my father. He was a great leader, and he was in charge all the time. I also knew this solemn fact: nobody could whip my dad. He could stand up to anybody in the world. I respected my dad for his incredibly hard work, for his love for us, and for his strength.

My father communicated affirmation and love, but not with physical expressions. My mother hugged me plenty of times, but my dad never hugged me in his life. I remember sitting on my mother's lap when I was little and feeling close to her. Although we were not a physically affection-

Charlie and his parents, about 1928

ate family, each of us knew that Dad wouldn't hesitate to give his life for us—no questions asked. His strength and love provided a safe home. Dad wasn't a hugger, but he showed his love in other ways to make us feel special. We always knew we could count on him.

Our family took a vacation every year. We would leave around 9 o'clock in the morning to go to the County Fair, and we would stay until 9 o'clock that night. My brother and sisters and I were always excited, but when I got older I realized my dad didn't give two hoots about going to that County Fair. He would rather be working on the farm doing something constructive. Dad never took a real vacation in his life, and to my knowledge, he never took a day off. He worked all the time. Some people might think he would become bitter and narrow, but he enjoyed working. Providing for our family gave him purpose and meaning.

My mother was the essence of a lady. She was kind, consistent, and dignified. She carried herself with a quiet decorum that provided great stability for our family. In all of the hard work and the difficult times we had on the farm, I never heard her swear or even use a slang word. She was willing to give of herself in every situation to every person in her life. No sacrifice was too great for her.

My mother and father were a perfectly matched pair. My dad was always very generous. Occasionally, my mother thought he was a bit *too* generous for the good of the family—and she was probably right. But she never complained . . . not a single time. My mother had an amazing blend of consistency and optimism. What an incredible example to follow! In my entire life, I never remember her having a "down" day. If she ever felt depressed or sorry for herself, we never knew it. She always had a smile and a kind word, no matter how awkward the situation or how difficult the moment. I never had to worry, *I wonder how Mom will be feeling this morning,* or *I hope I say the right thing to Mom so she won't blow up at me.* I could always count on her being happy, smiling, and kind. To be honest, I've never met anyone quite like her. I hope some of her optimism has rubbed off on me.

Mom was incredibly industrious. She could get more done in an hour than most people did in a day. She often sliced potatoes to fry them for dinner. She could slice a potato almost as fast as you could look at it. It was unbelievable! She could fix a meal faster than anybody, and of course, my dad was always in a hurry because he had two or three jobs every day.

My mother's workday was grueling. She washed all our clothes on an old-fashioned scrub board, and I've seen her work in a garden for hours at a time, planting, weeding, pruning, and picking. My mother canned seven or eight hundred quarts of fruit and vegetables in a single season. Every year she put up a fifty-gallon barrel of dill pickles and a thirty-gallon barrel of sweet pickles. She picked wild blackberries and canned 150 quarts. She also picked and canned gooseberries, peaches, and

> She always had a smile and a kind word, no matter how awkward the situation or how difficult the moment.

apples. After we butchered the hogs, she rendered the fat, and we got the cracklings from the process. She made lye soap from the fat, then she canned the meat. My dad made sorghum molasses in the fall, and Mom canned a lot of it. In the winter she made biscuits from scratch every morning, cooked in a wood stove. She baked bread three times a week: Monday, Wednesday, and Friday. With no microwaves, no TV dinners, and no convenience stores, Mom was a busy woman!

One of the secrets to my mother's incredible attitude and stamina was that she would take a nap during the day if she got tired. But after 20 minutes or so, she was ready to go again. At night, after all of us had finished our chores, she read to us. We really enjoyed that time together. The last book she ever read made a big impression on me. It was a Civil War story, *Young Captain Jack.*

My mother had no understanding whatsoever of people who were sullen, bitter, or cranky. She chose to be positive every minute of every day, and she thought everybody else could be upbeat, too. I don't remember any whining among us children when I was growing up. In fact, being "down" or upset wasn't even discussed around our house. We didn't have time to whine. We were too busy having fun, doing chores, and helping Mom and Dad.

My dad's outlook on life was just as positive as Mom's. I don't remember a time in his life when he used the word *discouraged.* He had plenty of reasons to get discouraged, but he refused to let those things get him down.

A case in point took place when I was about 13. Wilbur was with Dad one day when Dad's right hand got caught in a cane mill, which ground his little finger completely off. His next three fingers were very badly cut. Back in those days on a farm, medical care was very primitive. Because his hand was so mangled, his thumb was reattached awkwardly so that his thumbnail was on the palm side of his hand. He lost a lot of blood.

This accident happened in the fall, and for two months we wondered if Dad would live. In 1936 and 1937, times were tough all over the country, but they were especially hard on our farm with Dad's hand and health so fragile. That winter, after we finally were convinced he was going to make it, he asked us to help him shuck corn. His wound wasn't healed yet, and his right hand was still in a sling, but he wasn't one to complain or to avoid work. Dad put the corn between his knees, scraped off the shuck with his legs, and used his left hand to jerk it and snap it off. Shucking corn took us several days. One of those nights I walked by my parents' bedroom and saw Dad taking off his pants. On the inside of both legs were the most horrible sores I've ever seen in my life. The corn had rubbed all the skin off. Yet Dad never said a word. In fact, he went to the barn the next day and shucked corn just as he had done the days before—by holding it between his legs and pulling it to get the shuck off. That had to hurt so bad! But he was working for our family's benefit . . . and he never complained.

When I saw this kind of commitment to us, my already high admiration for my father went through the roof. My

With Mrs. Gould and classmates, seventh grade

dad used to say, "You haven't lost until you quit." He had some terrible things happen to him, but he just kept going.

Many times over the years, I've thought of the examples my mother and father set for me. When faced with difficult times, I've never even thought of quitting. My parents' consistency, optimism, tenacity, and refusal to complain shaped my life in ways that are profoundly positive. I only hope I have been—and will be—that same kind of influence on others around me. That is a legacy to be proud of.

When I was a boy, most of the kids in school had only one pair of bib overalls. At night their mothers had to wash their overalls and hang them up to dry so they could be worn again the next day. But I always had two pairs of overalls. My dad worked very hard to be sure he provided for his children. When he got his farming done each day, he worked for somebody else to make some more money. A dollar a day was the going rate for farm labor in those days.

One day a neighbor called my dad and said, "Norval, if you come and help me, I'll give you $1.25 a day because you are a lot better help than most men around here." My dad never forgot that—and neither did I. To think that someone would give him an extra 25 cents a day because he worked so hard! At the end of the six-day week, Dad had earned $7.50 instead of only $6. We could go to the grocery store and buy all the groceries they had for that much money! We also took our cream and eggs to market to make a little extra. These were the darkest days of the Depression, yet Dad made sure our family lived well. Many people didn't have enough to eat, but my dad cared for us and provided for our needs. When I talk about my father working so hard, people sometimes wonder if I felt abandoned as a child. No! I knew my dad was coming home every night, and that he would be there the next morning. Because of him, our family always felt very secure.

We got electricity at our house in 1941 when I was fourteen years old. That was quite a day! I got home after school, and there was a cord hanging down from the middle of the ceiling with a light bulb dangling at the end. If you pulled the chain, the light came on. It seemed like a miracle! It was the most fantastic thing I'd ever seen. Previously we had used kerosene lamps, requiring us to trim the wicks, fill them up with oil, and wash the globes. But now that we had electricity, we had entered the modern age.

Not long after we got electricity, my dad bought my mother a washing machine—a Maytag washer with wringers. My mother was overwhelmed! For one of the few times I can remember, she had tears in her eyes. Dad was so proud. He knew that this 45-year-old woman had used a scrub board all her life. Soon after that, Dad bought her a refrigerator. From that day on, we didn't have to hang our milk down in the well to keep it cool. And at about the same time, Dad bought a radio for us. What a time in our family! We had electricity, a refrigerator, a washing machine, and a radio. What more could we ask for?

One of my sisters was named Thelma Dee, but we all called her just Dee. She was three and a half years older than I was, and she and I fought terribly! She teased me, and of course, I got mad at her. Yet even when my anger

Tenth grade

flamed at her for picking on me, I got over it quickly. Whenever we were apart, we missed each other very much. And as soon as we got back together, she would start teasing me again and more arguments followed. She and I had a special relationship. It sometimes looked like we stayed angry at each other all the time, but underneath all the teasing, we genuinely loved each other. As I grew older and bigger, I got stronger. One day I hurt Dee in one of our scuffles. She cried—which was something she didn't do very often. I felt so bad! I said, "I will never ever do that again." Our scuffles were a way of showing affection, but when I hurt my sister, I resolved that I would never let my temper get the best of me again! To this day, I still remember how badly I felt that day when I hurt Dee.

My brother Wilbur was nearly eleven years older than me. He always looked after me, and I loved and respected him. I now realize what a pain it must have been to have a little brother like me following him around all the time, but he never complained. He was a great guy. Later, when we were both grown men, Wilbur prayed for me regularly and fervently. Even at a very early age, he was a hero to me.

My family didn't have much of a spiritual life. We rarely went to church, though I occasionally went with friends as a young person. God was not a topic of conversation in our home. My dad didn't curse or drink, and he was one of the most ethical men anyone ever met. In fact, a devout Christian could not be more ethical than my dad. He was the kind of person who always was looking out for other people. He helped everybody and anybody who needed help.

On many, many occasions, my dad stopped to pick up people who were stranded on the side of the road. I remember him stopping his Model A or Chrysler or Packard to give the man a ride. Invariably, Dad rolled down his window and asked, "What are you doing?"

The man usually looked both embarrassed and hopeful when he replied, "Nothing."

Dad then nodded toward the door and said, "Get in. You look like you could use a good meal."

The man's eyes lit up as he opened the back door and flung his meager belongings on the back floorboard and hopped in. But my dad didn't just bring the man home for a meal. He offered to let him stay all winter with us! (This happened almost every winter my entire childhood, especially during the Depression years.)

These men became part of our family. They worked for us doing chores around the farm, and my mother washed their clothes and cooked for them. My dad gave them a little spending money to help them out. Sometimes, we had two people living with us. That was my dad's way: he was incredibly generous. My mother never said a word about it. Dad's generosity to these men was fine with her.

> But my dad didn't just bring the man home for a meal. He offered to let him stay all winter with us!

We didn't have a big house, so all of us had to make adjustments. Nobody seemed to mind. Dad's attitude seemed to permeate all of us, and everybody in the family welcomed these people. They sat at the table and ate with us just like they were relatives. Sometimes the children had to share a bed so the man who was living with us would have his own bed—and his own room—to sleep in.

One man who stayed at our home was named Steiner. He was an older man by my standards—older than thirty! We also kept a man by the name of Ed Brainerd, who stayed with us several different times. He was a stocky man with gray hair, and not too tall. Mr. Brainerd was getting pretty old, so he really appreciated Dad giving him a warm place to live during the bitter cold of the Missouri winter months. Nobody asked my father to invite these men to come to our home. It was entirely his idea.

In that same spirit of generosity, my dad often loaned people money. He didn't have much money himself, but he was willing to help people in need. At one point, my uncle broke his leg in a horse race. The horse couldn't make a turn and hit a tree, and the impact almost tore my uncle's leg off. My uncle needed some financial help, but this was long before any insurance was available. Dad sold him some land so he could farm and carried the entire amount to help my uncle get on his feet again—financially and literally.

Dad helped people continually. I can remember my mom smiling and saying, "Norval, you keep on, and we are going to end up in the poorhouse." Of course, we never did. God rewards the generous, even if those generous people aren't believers yet.

In the past few years, God has allowed me to be a part of helping people who are in need. The Lord gave me a vision to minister to struggling young people, and in the past few years, that vision has taken shape. This vision includes ministering to every aspect of their lives, through education at our school, love and accountability in homes or at the Recovery Center, Christ-centered instruction and prayer, and building discipline as they work at the dairy. We call this place Heartland. This part of the country is called "The Heartland of America," but even more than that, we gave it that name because our ministry is designed to change people's hearts. We bring young people to Heartland who need a fresh start, and as God works in their lives, their direction is forever changed. Recently I told a friend some stories about my Dad stopping on the side of the road to invite men to come to our home for a meal, for a night, or for a winter. As I told these stories, my friend told me, "Charlie, you're just like your Dad!"

> "Charlie, you're just like your Dad!"

I guess an apple doesn't fall far from the tree.

With high school friends, in graduation robes, 1945

CHAPTER 2

A FEW GOOD MEN

When Japan bombed Pearl Harbor and our country went to war, I was fourteen and Wilbur twenty-five. Our family expected him to be drafted, but he was married and had a baby, so he was never called. As the war progressed and the need for men intensified, the draft boards began calling married men—even those with children—to meet their quotas. But by that time Wilbur was twenty-eight, and the draft boards didn't want men who were that old.

I was desperate to get into the fighting. When I was fifteen, my cousin, Dewey Sharpe, and I conspired to join the Navy. One morning when we were supposed to go to school, Dewey and I hitchhiked to the recruiting office in Quincy, Illinois. Our stint in the Navy didn't last very long. We told them we were eighteen years old, but the induction officer scowled, "Let me see your birth certificates." When we couldn't produce them, he turned us over to the police. The police called my dad and told him what we'd done. I felt like a criminal.

My dad drove down to the police station after midnight. When he walked through the door, I would rather have seen Satan himself! I hadn't even left a note to tell my parents I had gone off to fight for democracy. The first thing they knew about our leaving was when the police called. While we sat waiting, I felt ashamed for running away, but when I saw Dad walk through that door, I suspected that shame wasn't the worst thing I'd be feeling!

Dad didn't say anything to me when he came in. He just walked to the desk and signed some papers. The policeman nodded to us, then Dad motioned for us to head for the door. We walked outside and got in the car. I was ready for the bomb to go off, but to my surprise, Dad never said a word on the way home. The drive lasted about an hour—a very long hour! As we neared our house Dad broke the silence. He said, "Boys, I want to tell you something. Home is not a bad place." That was all he ever said. He never, ever said another word about that day. I said to myself, *You know what? That's a fact! Home looks pretty good to me. I'm glad to see it!* I think Dad must have appreciated our desire to serve our country . . . even though our zeal was a bit misplaced. I respected and loved my Dad even more for the way he handled that situation with Dewey and me.

When I graduated from high school in the spring of 1945, I planned to do two things: get married and go into the service. It seemed that everybody I knew got married when they got out of high school back in those days—85

Charlie and Wanda dating, 1945

percent of our graduating class was married within that year. I married my high school sweetheart, Wanda, and then

> When I graduated from high school in the spring of 1945, I planned to do two things: get married and go into the service.

I joined the Marine Corps. The war in Europe had just ended in May, but the Allied forces expected heavy fighting as they anticipated the invasion of Japan. I was sent to Parris Island, South Carolina, for boot camp. After being there about three weeks, Wanda wrote and informed me, "I think I'm pregnant." I couldn't believe it, but it was true. I was going to be a dad!

The atomic bombs were dropped on Hiroshima and Nagasaki in August of 1945 while I was at Parris Island. Shortly after that, the Japanese emperor surrendered. The war was over. After boot camp, my regiment was sent to China where a civil war was raging between Mao's Communists and Sun Yat Sen's Nationalist Chinese. We were stationed about a hundred miles south of Beijing in Tensing, and we were put on high alert several times. My regiment guarded Japanese prisoners captured by the Allied Forces. These prisoners were demoralized. We had to watch them very closely because many of them tried to commit suicide. In their culture, surrender was worse than defeat, so these men were humiliated. Stripped of honor and dignity, many of them believed the only acceptable way to respond was to kill themselves by committing hara-kiri, thrusting a knife into their stomachs and disemboweling themselves.

One day in Tensing, I was on the second floor of a building talking to others in our outfit. We had the window open. Down on the street, two American Marines were walking by. They heard my voice, and one of them turned to the other and said, "That sounds just like Charlie Sharpe!" They ran up the stairs and into the room where I was. To my surprise, there stood my cousin, John Sharpe, and a long-time friend, Delbert Myers! Both men were from LaBelle, Missouri. Until that moment, I had no idea they were stationed in China, and they had no idea I was there. What a small world!

The Japanese people put everything they had into that war. They really didn't have very much equipment. Japan is a relatively small island nation with few natural resources. For many years before the war, they bought thousands of shiploads of scrap iron from the United States, and they built almost all of their war machinery—tanks, planes, guns, and ships—out of American scrap iron. Japanese soldiers were known for their incredible fighting spirit, but much of their equipment was inadequate or obsolete. We saw Model A cars that had been armor-plated to serve as tanks! I don't know how those people thought they could win the war against America with equipment like that. I specifically recall standing in Tienamen Square in Beijing, China, at the end of the war and thinking what a wonderful thing it is to be an American. I was so proud because, with the other Allied Forces, we had won a worldwide, two-front war against what had been the strongest military machines on the planet.

After a few months in Tensing, I volunteered to serve at the U.S. embassy in Beijing. It had been closed since early in the war when Japan invaded China. Like other Marines, I couldn't imagine the Communists taking over the country, but Mao was determined to seize control. The Marines pulled out in 1946, and shortly after that, the Communists took over. I believe the United States and the Allied Forces made a mistake in not fighting Mao and his troops. If we had stayed there and fought, the Communists wouldn't have conquered the world's most populated country.

I enjoyed military service, and I would have reenlisted if I had not been married, but I needed to get home and take care of my family. My son Rodney was born six months before the end of my tour of duty in September of 1946. Wanda had sent me some pictures, but that wasn't enough. To say the least, I was excited about getting home to see Wanda and hold that little boy in my arms.

I took the train as far as I could, and I got a ride the rest of the way home. Wanda knew I was in the States, but she didn't know exactly when I would arrive. I saw her walking from the mailbox to the house, which was almost half a mile. Our car pulled up next to her as I leaned out the window and said, "Hey, would you like to have a ride?" She almost dropped over when she realized it was me!

The homecoming went very well. It was wonderful to see Wanda and little Rodney. The next morning, I went to work with my dad cutting cane. I enjoy working and being productive, so it was easy to revert to the routine of working six days a week.

I went into the construction business later that fall, working for a local contractor. The next year I bought a piece of equipment and worked on my own for a while. Occasionally people asked me to help them with construction projects. Later I began to get contracts from large companies. I thoroughly enjoyed the construction business. Our family grew just as fast as the business. By the time I was twenty-three, Wanda and I had three children: Rodney, Linda, and Carol.

In the Marines, 1946

LEARNING TO GET ALONG—NO MATTER WHAT!

When I was in the Marine Corps, I learned a great lesson on human relations. I got to the huge, military induction center in St. Louis and went through the process with hundreds of other young men. Among them was a young man with snow white hair. He and I ended up in the same unit, and of course, we called him "Whitey." I have no idea what his real name was; the only thing anyone called him was his nickname.

Whitey was one of those people—and there have been very few of them in my life—whom I instantly detested. I tend to instinctively like people, and I can count those on one hand who are exceptions. Whitey was cocky—a very, very arrogant young man—and a wisecracker. No matter what I said, he responded with a sarcastic remark. I tried to ignore the guy because I thought we would soon be going in different directions. The war in Europe was over, so the odds were that Whitey and I would be sent from the induction center to different boot camps to train to secure the peace our soldiers had won. I would be glad to be rid of him!

> Whitey was one of those people—and there have been very few of them in my life—whom I instantly detested.

I got my assignment for boot camp: Parris Island, South Carolina. I boarded the train, and there was Whitey in the same car. He and I rode all the way to Parris Island together, and when we got assigned to our barracks, Whitey was in the bunk directly above me. I thought, *This is ridiculous! I can't get away from this guy!*

Boot camp lasted twelve weeks. It was a period of incredibly rigorous physical training, intense mental preparation, learning the rules of engagement, and finding out how to get along under pressure with others in cramped quarters. At the time, my main enemy wasn't the Japanese or the Germans. It was Whitey! He and I had quite a few run-ins during boot camp. I was getting tired—really tired—of his lip. We tried to stay away from each other, but in that environment we were with each other all day, every day. To be honest, I don't think he liked me any better than I liked him. We had a heated war of words, and from time to time we almost came to blows.

When we finished boot camp, we didn't get a leave. We were each immediately assigned to a unit and shipped out to points across the globe. There was a very good chance I would never see most of these men again . . . except Whitey. He and I were put in the same unit bound for China.

We took a train north to the naval base at Norfolk, Virginia, where we joined 8,000 other troops and crew on the USS *Wakefield*, an antiquated World War I German luxury liner that had been captured by the Allied Forces and converted into one of the biggest troop transports in the Navy. It was a great old ship that was incredibly fast. It could do 40 knots. I walked up the gangway and found my assigned compartment among the hundreds on the ship. I lay down on my bunk, and after a few minutes, Whitey came in the door and settled into the bunk right above me! Some of the compartments could accommodate as many as seven bunks high . . . and out of 8,000 men, Whitey was assigned to the bunk directly above me. By now, I suspected this wasn't a coincidence.

The *Wakefield* took us through the Panama Canal and on to Pearl Harbor. At that time, the Navy hadn't removed any of the ships that had been sunk in the surprise attack almost four years earlier. It was an eerie, ghostly, ghastly sight! We saw the remains of the *Arizona* where it was sunk. And Whitey was still with me at every turn, spewing out sarcasm and insults with no apparent provocation.

We stopped at Pearl Harbor for only four hours. After that brief liberty, we got back on the ship. I climbed in my bunk, and Whitey was only inches above me again. Our trip to China lasted a total of thirty-one days. Finally, we sailed into the shallow water of the Yellow Sea. The *Wakefield* drew about forty feet, so we had to go ashore on landing craft. As I got my position on the landing craft, I looked up. Whitey was standing next to me. After all this time, we still despised the sight of one another!

Our unit took the train to Tensing, China. Whitey was assigned, of course, to the same car I was in. When we arrived in Tensing, he and I were assigned to the same barracks. The brass assigned us to the same work detail. The number on our dog tags was almost identical, so the Marine Corps put us together for every event, every transport, and every detail. We were not only in the same

platoon, we were almost in the same bed! Day in . . . day
out . . . Whitey and Charlie, always together.

One day an officer asked for volunteers to go to Beijing
for a special assignment. I wanted to see the capital, and I
sure wanted to get away from Whitey, so I instantly volun-
teered. I hate to admit it, but getting away from that guy was a prime motivation for me. I couldn't stand his smart mouth

We were not only in the same platoon, we were almost in the same bed!

anymore! I hadn't been able to shake Whitey since the St.
Louis induction center. Now I finally had the opportunity.

I took the train to Beijing and was assigned to a detail
at the embassy. Life was good! A new, exotic city, an exciting assignment—and no Whitey! But only a few days later,
Whitey and a few other men showed up. I couldn't believe
it! Whitey and I were together again. I might have thought
it was a bad joke, but to tell the truth, it wasn't all that funny.

By this time, the soldiers and sailors who had been in
the war for a while were being discharged. After several
months in Beijing, those of us who joined at the end of the
war were being sent home, too. All of the married men were
going to get discharged, so it was my turn to go. I was told
to pack my clothes and take a train to the coast. Three ships
comprised our convoy; I was on the smallest of the three.
When I boarded the ship, there was Whitey! I don't know
how a single guy like Whitey was authorized to be shipped
home with us married men. It didn't make sense, but still,
there he was again.

The armed forces called these "victory ships," but we called them "Kaiser's Coffins" because they were built without rivets. The seams were only welded. In a big storm, we envisioned the seams ripping apart and all hands going down together—not an encouraging thought when you're in a cramped compartment several decks down in the middle of the ship. And Whitey was in the same compartment with me. I saw him every day.

Out at sea, our skipper sailed us through one of the worst typhoons to ever hit the Pacific. For several days, he couldn't get us out of it! The intense wind and waves kept driving us backward. One day we made just one knot—only a bit over one mile per hour! The ship was creaking and groaning above the sound of the storm. Those of us down below thought the seams might rip at any minute. Obviously, we weren't the only ones who were worried. At one point, we were given orders to stand by to abandon ship. It was a hair-raising experience, and Whitey was with me!

We finally sailed past the storm. The rest of the two-week voyage was relatively uneventful, and we were glad to reach the port of San Diego. We Marines got on board a troop train going to Great Lakes Naval Station for discharge. Whitey—along with his ever-acid tongue—was on the train with me.

Our trip across the country lasted three or four days because the train made frequently stops. If any freight or passenger trains were going the other way, we had to pull off to the side. At the naval station, Whitey and I checked out together. I was now sure this would be the last time I saw him, so I shook his hand and wished him well.

During all these months of being constantly sandpapered by Whitey's sarcasm and cockiness, I had realized his continual presence wasn't an accident. Being assigned to be with a guy like this over and over again couldn't just happen by chance. Hundreds of times during those months, I thought, *Somehow, there is a lesson in this for me.*

The moral to the story is that you have to learn to be content with what you have. No matter who you are with, no matter how difficult the situation, you have to rise above it and have a positive attitude. To be honest, I'm not sure I applied that lesson very well during my time with Whitey, but it was a lesson I have remembered all the rest of my life.

> No matter who you are with, no matter how difficult the situation, you have to rise above it and have a positive attitude.

The apostle Paul certainly had a wide range of experiences. He saw thousands respond to the gospel. He built strong churches. And sometimes he was viciously attacked by religious leaders and suffered tremendous hardships. In all these situations, he learned to be consistently content. He wrote to the Philippians:

> For I have learned to be content whatever the circumstances. I know what it is to be in need, and I know what it is to have plenty. I have learned the secret of being content in any and every situation,

whether well fed or hungry, whether living in plenty or in want. I can do everything through Him who strengthens me. (Philippians 4:11-13)

You have to learn to not let people agitate you. If you let them get under your skin and control your attitude, they can destroy you! In this life you may be able to control a few things, but you can't usually control people or circumstances. You can, however, still experience peace and contentment.

My relationship with Whitey showed me—clearly and often—that I can't control every aspect of my life. And when I can't control things, I need to make the best of them. I never enjoyed being with Whitey, but toward the end of our time together, I was not as frustrated and agitated by his antics. That's some progress, at least. This experience with Whitey challenged me to learn to get along with people. No matter how bullheaded they may be, I need to accept them. I see how people affect other people every day. Some people naturally get on each other's nerves, but I don't let it affect me as much anymore. Instead of being repulsed by such people, I have learned to look for a deep need in their lives. We can condemn their obnoxious behavior, or we can see an opportunity to minister to them. If we say, "I'm going to get away from that person. I don't care what I have to do, but I'm out of here," our selfishness blocks any opportunity to communicate the love of God. We can look at every person—no matter how awkward, sarcastic, or withdrawn—as someone who needs the love of Jesus from us.

Charlie and Wanda, 1949

Chapter 3

Foundations

My brother Wilbur became a Christian back in the 1930s. He didn't bug me, but from time to time, he asked, "Charlie, why don't you come to church with me?"

I always told him, "One of these days, I will." But I really didn't intend to go to church. I was just putting him off.

We noticed a big change in Wilbur's life after he became a Christian. He was very intent about his faith, and Christ became his highest priority. Wilbur wasn't a Christian just on Sunday—he lived it every moment. His commitment made us uncomfortable because he constantly talked about the Lord. Even though I wasn't a religious person at all, I always knew there was something real about Christ. So when Wilbur invited Wanda and me to church for the thousandth time, we finally agreed to go. At this point, Wilbur had been a Christian for ten or twelve years.

That day in February of 1947, the pastor preached an old-time "hellfire and brimstone" sermon. He seemed to dangle me over the pit of hell so I could almost feel the heat. I thought, *I don't want to go there! I've got to get up and give my life to the Lord. I could die and go to hell if I don't!*

This was not the first time I had heard the gospel. I had heard the Good News a few times earlier in my life, but for some reason, it hadn't sunk in. In the church I grew up in, they didn't preach salvation or present the gospel. From what I heard there, I didn't even know a person could get saved. Yet when I went to church with Wilbur, the gospel message was clear and strong. I felt the tremendous burden of my sin! I remember feeling, *I'm wrong, and I'm a sinner. I can't go to heaven if I don't repent. I'd better do it now!*

Wanda and I went to the altar together. In those days, people bowed before God when they went to the altar. They didn't stand and say, "I accept Christ." People got saved on their knees. Wanda and I kneeled and trusted in Christ to be our Savior and Lord. I'll never forget that moment. It was a fantastic experience! I felt total relief—the burden of sin was gone!

In the days that followed, I could sense Satan attacking me with doubt, saying, "You're just fooling yourself, Charlie. Nothing happened to you. You're not really a Christian at all!" I was in Illinois looking for some machinery to start farming when those doubts flooded my mind. My heart and my stomach were both in knots as I wrestled with truth and doubts. Finally, I couldn't stand it any longer. I stopped my car and got down on my knees on the floorboard in the front seat. I cried out, "Lord, if You're real, show me!" At that moment, an overwhelming and undeniable peace came over me. That was over fifty years ago, but I still remember it like it was yesterday. After that moment on the floorboard of my car, I never again doubted my experience with the Lord.

> I'll never forget that moment. It was a fantastic experience! I felt total relief—the burden of sin was gone!

Unfortunately, I didn't let the grace of God penetrate very deeply into my life or my relationship with Wanda. At the time I thought I was doing just fine. But in retrospect, I was not the caring husband I should have been. I let selfishness erode our love from time to time. Instead of sacrificing for each other, we tended to compete against each other, resulting in both of us frequently feeling slighted by the other. Competition is a poor substitute for love in a family. I wish I had shown the love and affirmation Wanda wanted and needed, the love that Christ wants all husbands to show their wives. But I didn't. I can offer no excuses for not being the husband I should have been.

With this hindsight, I can now see many people who think they are doing fine, yet their lives and their most important relationships are shallow, empty, and heartless. They need someone to care enough to tell them the truth. Sometimes the truth hurts, but it always can heal. That's what Heartland is all about—healing truth.

My work in the construction business grew and prospered. I became a superintendent of a paving company, the top man in the field. I made a good living in this line of work. During my last year in the construction business, I made $22,000, which was a lot of money in 1961. In those days, a new car cost $3,000, and a new three bedroom home sold for $18,000. I made a good living, but I realized my life was going nowhere. I was ready for a new career. Looking back now, I can see that the Lord was already setting the stage for what I was to do with my life.

Wilbur and I started preaching at the same time, but we still worked full-time to support our families. Wilbur had a meat processing plant for the rural area so the farmers could bring their hogs and cattle to have them butchered. I had been in Chicago operating heavy equipment for a construction job we had just finished. In the winter, outdoor construction came to a halt, so our entire crew was out of work for several months. My co-workers all went to apply for unemployment, but I certainly didn't want to do that. I got home on a Saturday night, and I went to see my brother. I told him I was out of work for a while, and he said, "Charlie, do you want to work?"

I said, "Sure, I do! I don't want to sit around doing nothing."

Wilbur told me, "Well, come by my place on Monday and you can cut meat."

Early Monday morning, I showed up. Wilbur put a side of beef on the table and nodded to me to get to work. I grabbed a knife and a saw, and began my career as a meat packer. After several days of cutting and packing meat, Wilbur said, "Charlie, we haven't talked about money."

I responded, "No, we haven't. Just pay me whatever you think is fair."

He asked, "What about $65 a week?"

I answered, "Sounds good to me."

Unemployment paid $65 a week, so my friends laughed at me and said, "Charlie, why don't you apply for unemployment? You're crazy to work for the same amount of money we get for doing absolutely nothing!"

I told them, "Don't worry about me. I'd rather be working than sitting around doing nothing . . . even if the pay is the same."

I worked all winter cutting meat with Wilbur, and I enjoyed working with him. When spring rolled around and it was time for the construction jobs to gear up again, my buddies were sad because they were going to have to go to work. I was glad to go back to operating heavy equipment and making more money, but I sure wasn't sorry to have worked for Wilbur that winter.

I had a wonderful experience as I began to trust Christ. In those first years of my faith, I grew spiritually and I was zealous for God. As I studied the Scriptures, prayed, and talked to anyone who would listen about Christ, God used me to lead some people to repentance and to encourage some who had lost hope. I was thrilled that God would use me like this. Gradually, I began to sense that God just might be calling me into the ministry as a bivocational pastor. That idea began as a faint thought, but it grew and strengthened into a heartfelt desire. I talked to Wanda and Wilbur and several others, and they all encouraged me to take that step.

I was still in the construction business when I was ordained as a minister of the gospel, and I started a church near where Heartland is today. Our first service had a congregation consisting of my family, a mother, and her two daughters. The mother was in her 70s, and her daughters were in their 50s. But it was a beginning.

Before long, our congregation grew to about 125 to 150 people, and we built a new building. I enjoyed seeing God's hand at work in our family of faith. However, I became too busy, and that busyness very gradually began to affect my spiritual growth. I lost my desire to put God first, but the decline was so subtle that I didn't even recognize it until after I was bone dry.

I never planned to fall away from God. I didn't get up one morning and say, "I think I'll stop walking with God. I'm going to backslide today." I kept preaching and leading for a year even when I was running on empty, but I couldn't keep that up for long. I failed God, and I failed the people in that congregation. I thank God that the church is still active today in that same place. In many instances, young churches that lose their pastors struggle and die, but this one has continued to follow Christ. I regret that I didn't finish what I set out to do, but I'm not the kind of person to brood on the past and be consumed by it. I closed that book and moved on with my life.

> I lost my desire to put God first, but the decline was so subtle that I didn't even recognize it until after I was bone dry.

Charlie, Wanda, Carol and Rodney, 1952

After I left the ministry, I began selling insurance. God blessed my hard work and my integrity. I believe He blesses His righteous principles even when those who are following them are leading checkered lives. In this case, the principles were blessed more than I was.

I wasn't consumed with the desire for money. In fact, acquiring a lot of money was not a major motivator for me at all. I never cared to be the richest man in the cemetery, but I always wanted to be successful and accomplish a lot in my life.

It may be hard for some people to understand, but I believe God has seen me through all kinds of situations in my life—some that He wanted me to experience and some He didn't—in order to bring me to the life and ministry I have today. I might have remained a pastor, but in His grace, God took me beyond my sin and, in His providence, allowed me to accomplish His purposes in a different way.

For some, the calling of God into the ministry is clear and unmistakable, but I think others manufacture their own call. I believe God called me to the ministry, but I'm not convinced that is true of all preachers. In fact, I believe many preachers shouldn't be in the ministry at all. My calling was clear and strong, but I blew it.

God called me into the ministry, but I also believe God wanted me to leave the ministry when I did. The way I left didn't honor Him, but I think He wanted me to change course anyway. I wish I had been more responsive to God and His will, but He used other means to direct me out of the pastorate. The ministry we have today could never have taken place if I had stayed where I was. I only wish I had been more sensitive to God's leading at the time.

I really enjoyed our home and our children. My family, the construction business, and the ministry kept me very busy, but I never felt stressed at all because I enjoyed it so much. Rodney, Linda, and Carol were wonderful children, and I had a great time with them even though I don't think I was a very good dad. I loved them a lot, but I love them much more now than I did then. I provided for them, but the great tragedy of my life—something I am terribly ashamed about—is that after a point, my life was not consistent with the principles I tried to teach my children.

After a confusing period of life for all of us, it is one of the great miracles of God that they are now all serving Him. They didn't make that choice until I returned to the Lord. There's a message there, too. When I recommitted my life to Christ, God opened their hearts and drew them to Himself. The leadership of a father is so important. There's no way to overemphasize it. A father must lead in every way: in gentleness, in love, in compassion, and in strength. When he chooses to follow the Lord, God works in the hearts of his children, even if they have chosen destructive paths.

Almost three thousand years ago, the people of Judah were in trouble. Hezekiah was king, but most of his predecessors had drifted away from the Lord and the nation was beset by conquest and captivity. King Hezekiah, however, gave the people a promise of God's redemption. He wrote in a letter to all the people:

> If you return to the Lord, then your brothers and
> your children will be shown compassion by their
> captors and will come back to this land, for the Lord
> your God is gracious and compassionate. He will
> not turn His face from you if you return to Him.
> (2 Chronicles 30:9)

God's promise through King Hezekiah was realized by myself and my children three millennia later. Their turning to Christ has been among the most meaningful and fulfilling events in my life. I am deeply grateful to God for His mercy to them . . . and to me. But when my children were still young, I gave more attention to work than to God or my family.

One day a man named Basil Ferguson said to me, "Charlie, you ought to get into sales."

I was genuinely offended. I thought salesmen were charlatans. I responded, "Basil, you ought not to talk to me like that. I'm a decent person!" It had never occurred to me that sales make the world go 'round. Without sales, nothing happens. Without motivating people to take action, the world would be stagnant. I had never considered sales as a career before that day, and to be honest, the

"Charlie, you ought to get into sales."

thought took some time to sink in. My idea of work revolved around *producing* and *building*, not *talking* about the products to other people. And I was a hard worker . . . a very hard worker.

Basil was already in the insurance business, and he asked me to go to work in his company, Modern Security. I wrestled with that decision for several months. I loved construction. I was very good at my job. I was making a good living for Wanda and the children. Basil, however, kept asking me to sell insurance. I told him over and over again, "Basil, I can't do that. I'm in the construction business. That's what I'm good at doing, and I should stick with it."

The construction business looked wide open to me, and I felt secure in it. I knew I could get a job anywhere. But when it came to selling insurance, I sure didn't feel confident that I could make a living. It's frightening to think of how close I came to saying "No" to the insurance business. Like a lot of people, I didn't want to try something new and unproved, but I finally agreed to give it a try. I thought, *I'm going to do it, and then I'll know. Basil will leave me alone when he sees I've tried and I can't do it.*

This new career was a significant risk for me. Selling insurance was strictly on commission. I got no salary at all. Wanda had confidence that I could make a living in whatever career I chose. At the beginning, she had more confidence in me than I had in myself!

Basil sent me to a three-day introductory insurance school in Springfield, Missouri. Before leaving, I set up thirteen appointments for the days right after the school was over. I got out of school on Wednesday afternoon, and on my way back from Springfield that night stopped by for my first appointment with a cousin in Missouri. I walked in, sat down, and went through all the material I had just learned about the benefits of insurance. My explanation had all the details and enthusiasm of any new salesman, and I was convinced I was making a terrific, thoroughly convincing presentation. After listening to my eloquent delivery, my cousin frowned and shook his head. "Naw, Charlie. I don't think I need that." He walked me to the door and told me, "Thanks for coming. Good luck."

My career as an insurance salesman seemed destined to be a very brief and ignoble one. I couldn't even sell to my own cousin! I thought as I walked to the car, *It looks like I'm back in the construction business.* I knew I could get a good job building Interstate 80 near Moline, Illinois, and I seriously thought about going there the next morning. But I still had twelve other appointments over the next three days.

On Thursday I made the hard decision to go to my next appointment, and surprisingly, the man bought a policy. The next one did, too! And the third! Over those three days, every one of the twelve people bought insurance policies from me: twelve for twelve. I couldn't believe it! Maybe selling insurance wasn't such a bad deal for me after all.

My career in sales was off and running. I sold a policy every day for six months. I didn't work much on Sunday, but I often sold two policies on Saturday to make up the difference. Someone told me that my average of a policy a day set a national record. During the second six months, I averaged six policies a week. In that first year, I made more money than I ever dreamed of: $34,000. The second year I made $50,000, which is equivalent to at least $300,000 of purchasing power today. Before Basil began badgering me to go into sales, it had never occurred to me that I could make that kind of money.

The company asked me to take over a region of the state and to hire other salesmen. One of those I hired was John Cantrell. John and I became close friends, and I helped him stay in the business when he felt like quitting. One day he called me and said, "Charlie, I have sold policies to everybody I know. I can't sell any more. I'm going back to the feed business."

> I couldn't believe it! Maybe selling insurance wasn't such a bad deal for me after all.

I was flabbergasted. I reacted, "John, what are you talking about? You *haven't even started* selling insurance!"

I invited him to go with me on some calls the next day so I could cheer him up and put some steel into his backbone. That morning the weather was terrible—sleet, snow, and wind—but I picked John up and we started driving down the road. We noticed a man standing in the middle of a junkyard, and to John's surprise, I pulled in. I asked the man to get into the back seat of my car, and in the next few minutes, we sold him three policies that netted us a sales commission of $700, which would be paid annually . . . from a junkyard. John Cantrell was so excited he almost had a heart attack!

I loved selling insurance, but my passion for sales began to take a toll on my marriage. I moved to St. Joseph to manage the business, and I came home only on weekends. I hoped this arrangement would work well, but Wanda and

I grew increasingly distant. Our icy relationship was a strain. I filled that hole in my heart with the fulfillment of selling insurance, making a good living, and being promoted in the company. These proved to be poor substitutes.

In November of 1963, my second year at Modern Security, I had an idea for a new product. It was a brainstorm, an insight given to me by God that could revolutionize the insurance industry. I noted that at the turn of this century, the average life span of a man was only 41 or 42. Today, at the turn of the millennium, average life span is almost 80 years. The insurance industry was designed for people who died prematurely, and it provided for people who were left behind. It was appropriate and necessary in its time, but as people live longer, they need different coverage. Instead of death benefits for survivors, people would increasingly need money for retirement. The industry had to adapt to these changing needs.

The concept that I feel came from God was to combine mutual funds and insurance. Half of a person's premium would go to insurance and half to mutual funds. This blend would provide death benefits if the person died prematurely, but would also provide retirement income if the person lived to old age.

An additional aspect of this new plan solved a dilemma for many people. Some policy holders experience a disability which prevents them from finishing the policy and reaping the benefits, so I wanted to include a disability clause that finishes the program in case the person can't work to pay the premium. The insurance company steps

Sharing the vision at an early Ozark sales meeting, 1964

in to continue paying the premiums. So this new concept would work for someone if he lived, if he died, or if he became disabled. This idea was the most phenomenal, new concept in insurance in many years.

I realized the insurance industry was antiquated and needed to change, but certain others didn't see things the same way. I was completely and absolutely dedicated to my employer, Modern Security. I wanted our company to be the leader in revolutionizing the industry, so I made an appointment with the president, Pat Jones (the father of Jerry Jones, owner of the Dallas Cowboys).

> This idea was the most phenomenal, new concept in insurance in many years.

I was confident and excited about this appointment with Pat. I was the top salesman in his company, so I was certain I would receive a good hearing. Pat's secretary let me in. He greeted me warmly, and I sat in the chair in front of his desk. I began, "Pat, I've got an idea, and I want you to listen to it. It will revolutionize our company!"

The concept was simple and profound, and it only took me about fifteen minutes to explain it to Pat. During this time, he listened patiently. When I finished, I waited for his enthusiastic response. Pat scowled a bit as he looked at me and shook his head, "Charlie, we don't need that. Let's just sell what we've got."

I was dumbfounded. I exploded, "Pat, we don't have anything worth selling!"

He didn't appreciate my forthright, honest opinion. He retorted, "Sure, we do! We have a product that has met people's needs for a long time. There's no need to change now." That was it—no need for any further discussion. The appointment was over.

I walked out of Pat's office with a sick feeling in my stomach. I was devastated! I knew my career with Modern Security was over. I knew the company was finished if it wasn't willing to adapt to the realities of the marketplace. Pat refused to look forward and chart a bold future for the company. I knew it wouldn't survive . . . and ultimately, I was right.

When I slumped into the driver's seat for the long drive back to northeast Missouri that day, I thought, *What am I going to do? Where can I get a job?*

I considered job possibilities with other companies. Some offered some hope; most looked like dead ends. At some point on that 250-mile drive, a bold thought struck me, *I'll know what I will do. I'm going to start an insurance company of my own.* The very thought startled me! It seemed like the most ridiculous idea that has ever come out of anybody's mind!

> At some point on that 250-mile drive, a bold thought struck me, *I'll know what I will do. I'm going to start an insurance company of my own.* The very thought startled me!

I drove up to John Cantrell's house on my way back from Springfield, and I told him, "John, I'm going to start an insurance company of my own."

John seemed surprised at first, but then he told me, "Put your plan together and let me look at it. Maybe I'll go with you."

In addition to John, I had also hired my cousin, Chet Sharpe, to work for Modern Security. I explained the new insurance concept to him, and he was interested in the new company. The three of us—John, Chet, and I—planned to meet at John's house in Quincy to talk about our plans. When I got there, I could see that something was wrong. The atmosphere was tense. It was obvious John and Chet had been talking and planning, and it was also obvious they knew I wouldn't like their conclusions. After a few minutes, John said, "Charlie, I've made up my mind. I'm going to be the president of our new company because I don't think you are morally fit."

John knew my marriage with Wanda was not going well, and he thought he could use that to take over the company before it began. The only problem was that I was as morally fit as he was. I looked him right in the eye and told him clearly, "John, you can't be the president of this company because I'm the president. I don't know what your plans are, but I know what mine are. I'm going to build this company into one of the great companies of this nation. I don't think that's your plan. If you want to be a company president, you'll have to find some other company. That slot is taken here."

John instantly backed off. He said, "Well, okay. If you feel that strongly about it, you can be the president. Chet and I will go along with you."

That was a big red flag, but I didn't see it at the time. Years later, the same flag would wave even more boldly. At that point I wouldn't be able to miss it because it threatened to wreck the company. God gave me a loud, clear signal, but at that point, I wasn't paying attention.

In early December, I had severe, debilitating headaches. I finally had to go to the doctor, who diagnosed a severe case of pericarditis, the inflammation of the tissue around the heart. Pericarditis is a major health problem. If it penetrates the pericardium and goes into the heart, it is often fatal. I was very ill with a fever of 104 degrees. The doctor put me in the hospital, and I was there two weeks. When I got out in early January, I was so weak that I couldn't work my normal schedule. At the time I was still with Modern Security.

At the end of February, I announced I was resigning from Modern Security. That same day I announced I was going to start a new company. My announcement didn't go over very well! I was their star salesman who had sold more policies than any other three people in the company combined. In an instant, my image went from hero to villain. All the "Atta-boys!" changed to accusations and condemnations. I wasn't surprised. It's human nature to attack someone who walks away to chart his own course. I didn't wish my fellow employees any harm at all. I didn't leave because I was angry at them, but I knew the direction I was headed didn't fit into the plans of Modern Security. Pat Jones had made that very clear to me.

I hired a lawyer who knew how to put together an insurance company, and we started filling out and filing the paperwork immediately. It was a huge undertaking, especially for someone still recovering from a major illness. The days were long and the details sometimes overwhelming, but we just kept plugging away until it was all done. And it wasn't all drudgery; we had some great encouragements along the way.

Like any other new business venture, we needed capital. I made a list of people to ask to invest in our new company, but before I could see any of them, I had to go to the dentist for my second appointment to complete a root canal. On February 26, 1964, I went into Dr. Kapp's office, sat in the chair, and said, "Doctor, you've got to get this finished. Today's the last day I'll see you."

He was surprised and asked, "What's the hurry, Charlie?"

"I'm starting an insurance company, and I won't have time to come back again."

He said, "You are? Well, I want to put some money into it."

I was surprised. "Dr. Kapp," I said, "I'll let you do that, but first I have to get my paperwork in order. I don't even have a name for the company yet."

Dr. Kapp wouldn't wait. He laughed, "That's okay! I'll give you some money even if I don't know the name of the company."

I still tried to talk him out of it, but he insisted that he put some money in my new company that very day. I had plenty of time to think as he excavated in my mouth, and I figured he would give me $1,000 or $2,000. After he finished my root canal, Dr. Kapp walked me to the front of his office. At the receptionist's desk, he told his bookkeeper to make out a check.

Again, I tried to stop him. "Dr. Kapp, I really don't want this money now."

He said, "Charlie, just take it and put it in the bank. When you get ready, you've got the money."

I thought, *Well, a couple of thousand dollars won't make much difference. I might as well take it to keep from offending him.*

The bookkeeper said, "How much and to whom, Dr. Kapp?"

He said, "Make it out to Charlie Sharpe—for $50,000."

I almost dropped my teeth . . . new root canal and all! I took the check and went straight to the United Missouri Bank in Kansas City. I asked to see Mr. Kemper (for whom The Kemper Arena was named), the chairman of the board.

Mr. Kemper listened patiently to my story, then I asked, "Sir, would you be our banker? We want to use your bank."

He said, "Yes, and I'll tell you what . . . I think I should put some money into this new company of yours."

I smiled, "Mr. Kemper, I'll be happy to let you do that." He wrote a check for $25,000.

The bookkeeper said, "How much and to whom, Dr. Kapp?"

He said, "Make it out to Charlie Sharpe—for $50,000."

I wanted to raise half a million dollars. Actually, we only needed $400,000, but I wanted to have plenty of capital and surplus. But before I even started to see potential investors on my list, I already had $75,000! Thirteen days later, doctors, dentists, bankers, and other people had invested all of the money we needed. In fact, I had to send some back because I had more than I needed.

Incidentally, Basil Ferguson named the company Ozark National Life. Basil had started me in the insurance business, so I wanted to give him a chance to be a part of Ozark. He turned me down because, he told me later, he didn't think I would ever make it. Two others, however, believed in my dream enough to join me. John Cantrell became the Executive Vice President and Chet Sharpe became the First Vice President of the company. I was the President. The company was a tremendous success story from its beginning.

I flew home the next morning on an Ozark Airlines flight, and Wanda picked me up. We stopped in Quincy, and I bought her two new dresses. One of them was a fine dress. I still remember what I paid for it — $80. The other one was $40. I was so excited about our future! I told Wanda, "I'll tell you what we'll do. We'll sell our furniture and buy a house in Kansas City. You can buy all new furniture. I've got everything ready to go."

Wanda said, "No, Charlie, I don't think so."

I was shocked. "What do you mean?"

She stated calmly and firmly, "I want a divorce."

"You what?"

"That's right. I want a divorce."

I said, "Of course, you don't!"

She looked at me and her eyes told me this was not a whimsical decision. She had thought about this long and hard, and her mind was made up. I hadn't made her the priority I should have, and we had drifted apart. If I had been all I should have been as a husband, the divorce would have never happened. To tell the truth, I wasn't even bitter or disappointed. By that time we were so distant from one another that I didn't even try to work things out. My dreams and desires had shifted to my new business, and now my tense relationship with Wanda wouldn't be a hindrance. I'm not proud of that perspective. It was wrong; I gave Satan a foothold by longing for success more than wanting a strong family. And Satan used that foothold to drive a wedge between Wanda and me—not a wedge of bitterness, but a wedge of apathy. Could our marriage have been saved? Of course. But I wanted to focus on my business, so I convinced myself that our relationship was beyond hope, making it much easier to walk away.

Our divorce didn't take long. It was finalized on the fourteenth of June. Less than two weeks later, Ozark National was in business. All these things happened in a whirlwind: the concept of a new kind of insurance, a major

> And Satan used that foothold to drive a wedge between Wanda and me—not a wedge of bitterness, but a wedge of apathy.

heart disease, leaving Modern Security, beginning Ozark National Life, and our divorce.

Events were steamrolling forward. We quickly recruited a fine group of salesmen, and we needed to train them to understand our revolutionary product. At the first Ozark insurance school, we had forty-one people, including the executive staff. As the day neared for these men and women to hit the streets and sell our policies, I had one item of business to finish.

On June 25, 1964, I went to the capital at Jefferson City to get our certificate to do business from The Missouri Insurance Commission. I walked in and the insurance commissioner, Mr. Duggins, said, "What can I do for you?"

I stated confidently, "I have come to get the certificate for Ozark National Life."

To my astonishment, this man leaned over and glared, "You will never get it."

I said, "Mr. Duggins, what do you mean 'I'll never get it'? I've got forty-one people in school, and I've got the capital raised. I've got everything set. What's the problem?"

He didn't answer my question. He only repeated, "We are not giving you a certificate."

I had to think fast. It would be a blow to the morale of our agents if there was any delay in their getting out on the streets to sell insurance for Ozark. Quickly, a plan gelled in my mind. I stared at Duggins and said firmly, "Mr. Duggins, I know something about Warren Hearns that will hit every major paper in this state tomorrow morning if you don't give me that certificate."

Mr. Duggins looked stunned. To make sure he understood, I repeated my promise. "I'm either going to walk out of here with my certificate, or I am going to tell the newspapers what I know."

He said, "Mr. Sharpe, sit here a minute."

About ten minutes later, he came back and said, "Here's your certificate."

Warren Hearns was running for governor, and I was bluffing at the time. But I found out later that Pat Jones contributed $50,000 to his campaign on the condition that he wouldn't give me that certificate. It was only a week or so before the primary, and the Democratic race for governor was hotly contested. Hearns couldn't afford any kind of publicity that might damage his chances.

I walked out of Duggins' office and breathed a sigh of relief! The next day, June 26, 1964, Ozark National Life opened its doors for business.

In the first few months, we sold a lot of policies. Our salespeople were excited about our product, and they confidently conveyed that excitement to their clients. We had plenty of competition, however. During that time, twenty-four new insurance companies were started in Missouri. Ozark National was the last of the twenty-four. There

> I walked out of Duggins' office and breathed a sigh of relief! The next day, June 26, 1964, Ozark National Life opened its doors for business.

were so many salesmen on the streets that they almost needed name tags just to keep from selling insurance to each other. (Incidentally, as of today, not another insurance company has been started in Missouri since Ozark opened its doors. And of those twenty-four, we are the only one which has survived intact. The others have either folded or have been acquired by other companies.)

In the early years of Ozark National, I was married to the company. After the divorce, I focused all my energies on making the business a success. I didn't play golf or go fishing; I didn't go on vacations or waste a minute of time. I was involved in every decision. As anyone can imagine, a new insurance company has heightened risks. We sold insurance all day, and we prayed all night that policy holders wouldn't die so we wouldn't have to pay a death claim. We used to laugh when we said that to each other, but there was a measure of truth to the statement.

Ozark was the first insurance company in history to ever show a profit in the first six months: $13,000 in the black. We were off and running. Our business philosophy was simple and effective: "keep costs down," and "everybody is a salesman." We didn't spend any money if we didn't have to spend it. Our expenses were incredibly low! And we never forgot the top priority of selling. Everyone in the company was expected to sell policies—especially me.

Whenever we sold policies, we looked for new salesmen to recruit. Before long we had over 100 without having to raid Modern Security to get them. In fact, very few employees followed us from there. Today we have 850 salespeople.

When we started Ozark, we paid very handsome dividends to the policyholders. In 1965, after we had been in business for a short while, I woke up in the middle of the night and realized that if we continued to pay high dividends, the company would go broke in five or six years! I walked into the office the next day and gathered our top people in my office to tell them we had to change our direction immediately. Of course, they resisted. They felt our policy was etched in stone. One of them said, "Charlie, we've told thousands of policyholders what we would do for them. We can't change now!"

I looked him in the eye and said, "We *have* to change. We don't have an option. We have to go back to each of our policyholders and explain that we made a mistake."

John Cantrell told me, "Charlie, we can't change. Our policyholders will think that we've lied to them."

"No," I replied, "we haven't lied to them yet. We've only made an error in calculation. But if we don't tell them now, we *will* be lying to them because now we know the truth. We simply have to do it, John."

When the board got wind of this, they came unglued! They said, "This will ruin the company. We can't go back to the policyholders like this!"

I explained, "The company will be ruined for sure if we *don't* go back to them, change things, and make it right." I assured them, "I'll take full responsibility."

I set up meetings with all our policyholders. I told them, "Folks, we've made an error. We can't do what we said we'd do, and we need to be honest with you about it."

An amazing thing happened. Clients told us, "We want to buy more insurance from you, and we will tell our friends to buy from Ozark because we see that this company will be honest when something is wrong." We had a huge surge of sales at that point. This was a fantastic lesson for our board and for our agents. The clients never had a problem with the change, but our people had to learn that customers trust you much more when you are honest with them. This was a lesson for me, too. This experience taught me that if something is wrong, you have to make it right—and make it right immediately. That is a principle for business, in families, and with God. If we sin, we need to make it right with God (and with anyone else we've offended) immediately.

> This experience taught me that if something is wrong, you have to make it right—and make it right immediately.

Tom Brandt

—32 years with Ozark National Life, currently a Regional Manager

I worked for a utility company called New Orleans Public Service in the late 60s, but my job there didn't pay very well. My wife and I had three children, and I was looking for something to help me make some extra money for the family. Hugh Wyatt had hired a good friend of mine named Ralph Backer, and Ralph suggested that I think about working for Ozark National Life on part-time basis. Ralph motivated me by showing me one of his paychecks! People obviously liked the insurance he was selling them.

I had several other job opportunities besides Ozark. For example, a friend was looking for someone to run a gas station on the weekends, but I love to fish and hunt, so I didn't want that job. The Ozark job looked very good to me, but I was also cautious. My brother has a Ph.D. in accounting and is a CPA. I asked him to check out Ozark National Life to see if it was legitimate. He came back and told me, "Tom, I can't find anything wrong with the company, but it is very young. I'd be very cautious about working for them."

I pressed him, "So you didn't find anything wrong with them?"

"No, they're clean."

That was all I needed to hear. I decided to work for Ozark part-time for a while. I enrolled in the three-day Ozark National Life Insurance School. Hugh and the others leading the school were so enthusiastic, and I left there excited about my future in the company. When I finished the school, I thought, "Those people are crazy. I'm going to sell insurance my way. It'll work a lot better than theirs." I set up a lot of appointments with friends and acquaintances who needed insurance like we offered. I had a lot of confidence that I would do well, but the first five people turned me down. I was so discouraged that I decided to quit, but before I gave it up for good, I decided to try an appointment the way Hugh and the Ozark trainers said to do it. (My only motivation was to prove they were wrong.) On my next appointment, I went through the plan with a couple just like our training had taught me. I made sure they were qualified, and I told them up front that I would ask them for a decision after I finished my presentation. I carefully explained our insurance program, and then I asked this couple for their answer. I said, "Ma'am, what do you think of this?"

She responded thoughtfully, "Well, I think it sounds really good."

I turned to her husband, "Sir, what do you think of it?"

He nodded, "Yes, it sounds good to me, too."

I waited for a few seconds, then he looked at his wife and said, "Honey, go get our checkbook."

I hated to admit I had been wrong about my sales technique—but I had been dead wrong. That appointment saved my career with Ozark National Life, and to this day, I value the training I received at the beginning of my career with the company.

About that time, Charlie came to a meeting with us at the Fountainbleu in New Orleans. I listened to Charlie tell us how excited he was about the product we were offering people. His way of doing business was different from anything anyone else was doing, and it offered incredible benefits to the people buying insurance and to us who sold the insurance. It sounded so good. In fact, I began to wonder if it sounded *too good to be true*. I decided to look very carefully for the crack, the flaw in the company, so for three months I analyzed every scrap of information and every conversation with Ozark's management to find anything remotely off base.

After three months, I couldn't find a thing wrong with Ozark. Hugh Wyatt held meetings for us salesmen on Saturday mornings at 6:30. In one of these meetings, I announced to Hugh that I wanted to work for Ozark on a full-time basis. My job as a residential sales representative for Public Service was safe and secure, but my opportunities there were limited. The company had three managers, and the only way for me to advance was for one of them to be fired or to die. But I had a problem: I liked these three guys! They were my friends, and I didn't want them to be fired or die for me to get a promotion. At my exit interview, they tried to convince me to stay with Public Service. I explained that my job with Public Service offered me almost no chance of advancement, but the possibilities were limitless with Ozark. They understood perfectly and told me, "We wish you great success in your new work." Even the people who wanted me to stay could see my job at Public Service had been a dead-end road.

I went home and told my wife that I was going to quit at Public Service and work with Ozark National Life full-time. She didn't say a word. That wasn't a good sign. When I told my mother, she cried and told me, "Son, you're crazy to leave a good company where you've worked for ten years to go sell insurance for a brand new company!" My dad agreed with her. My brother told me again to be very careful about working for such a young company. So . . . I didn't get a lot of encouragement from my family to work for Ozark! I was sure, however, that

the opportunity with Ozark was bigger than anything I had ever imagined in my life. I respected
Charlie, I believed in our product, and I knew I
would receive all the support and encouragement I
would ever need to be successful.

Hugh Wyatt provided great leadership for
Ozark National in the South. He gave me encouragement and the resources to do my job well. I'll
never forget what he did for me. In fact, everybody
in the company was glad to help everybody else in
any way and at any time. It was a unique experience to feel supported by so many people like that.

One of the ways Charlie supported all of us was
to go out into the field and go on appointments with
us. He wasn't one of those corporate executives who
told people what to do but stayed isolated in his
ivory tower office. No, Charlie was out there with
us, side by side, leading us by example. We always
knew Charlie Sharpe was in the battle with us, so
we never had to wonder if Charlie understood what
we were trying to do. He understood because he was
right there with us. I remember one day in particular, Charlie went with me to visit a lady near Baton
Rouge. She invited us into her living room where
we sat on her antique furniture. Like many antiques,
this furniture was terribly uncomfortable. And in
addition, we were seated far apart from one another.
As our presentation continued, I could see Charlie
fidget and squirm. He didn't like that chair, and he

didn't like being so far away from this lady. In a couple of minutes more, Charlie got down on his knees and laid out papers on the coffee table in front of this lady! He was connecting now. He told her, "Let me show you what we're talking about. . . ." He explained our insurance plan with all his usual enthusiasm—from his knees, shuffling papers and pointing to all the things he wanted her to understand. And in a few minutes, she bought a policy.

Over the years, Charlie has had many opportunities to sell the company and walk away with millions of dollars in his pocket. Most people would have sold and never doubted that decision for an instant, but Charlie refused to sell the company because he is so committed to all of us who work for him. We might have begun as his employees, but we have become his friends.

Charlie and John Cantrell

CHAPTER 4

BETRAYAL

For the next ten years, Ozark National Life experienced tremendous growth. People realized our concept made sense. They appreciated the combination of death benefits and retirement income, and thousands of people bought policies. And thousands of people referred us to their family and friends.

Ozark's stock was offered initially at two dollars per share. By the late 60s, it was selling at sixty-four dollars a share, and in some cases, even higher. In 1970 we put the company on the New York Stock Exchange, and we continued to see tremendous success because of the unique way we were structured. We were profitable in the first year, even though the industry average for break-even is five years. We paid fairly low commissions, and we held our expenses to a bare minimum. We had our priorities in order there. We didn't have many people in administration. Even today, Ozark has only about 100 people in our corporate office. A comparable company would have over 300, maybe even 400. That fact alone saves millions of dollars in overhead.

I quickly made some money because my stock had risen so dramatically, and I wanted to invest it. I have always had a fondness for land, and I enjoyed the construction business. When opportunities to invest in construction projects came along in the early 70s, I jumped at the chance. Several of us participated in building apartments near San Antonio, Texas. But before we could get the construction finished and the property sold, interest rates rose from 6% to 12%. Potential buyers first became skittish, then they bolted and ran. Suddenly, what looked like great investments turned into financial black holes that sucked money from me incessantly. As interest rates continued to climb, I had difficulty servicing my debt. I was getting into trouble— big trouble. I tried to keep the deal afloat long enough to sell the property and make some money (or at least not lose too much), but the months dragged on and on. My personal bank account was depleted, and I had no more credit to keep the deal going.

My financial predicament didn't compare, however, with the trouble caused by rumors being spread about me. Though I always kept my personal finances strictly separate from the company business, someone started a rumor that I had invested Ozark's money in the failing land deal in Texas.

In early 1975, a group of bankers called me from Minnesota. They said they wanted to buy Ozark National. At first I dismissed the idea, but as the specter of personal bankruptcy became increasingly a reality, I realized the state insurance commission wouldn't allow the president of an insurance company to experience personal bankruptcy and retain control of the company. I would be too vulnerable; too many things could go wrong. If I was forced into bankruptcy, I would have to step down.

> My financial predicament didn't compare, however, with the trouble caused by rumors being spread about me.

When the Minnesota bankers offered to buy Ozark, I told them, "I'm not interested. I will not sell the company." All my friends were in this company, and if I sold it, they would lose everything. I had the controlling block of stock. The bankers offered me $12 a share for my stock which by that time had declined to only $5 a share. (It wasn't such a good idea to go on the New York Stock Exchange after all.) I refused their offer, so they told me, "Name your price."

I still refused. They kept increasing their offer. Finally, they offered $15 a share for my block of stock. That would mean I could pay off all my debts in Texas, pay my taxes, and still have two million dollars in my pocket. My other alternative was to go broke. I replied, "I'm not going to sell my stock and betray my friends."

My attorney said, "Take it! You don't need friends when you have two million dollars."

I said, "I'm sorry, but I'm not going to do that. I'm not going to leave all these people behind!"

Soon a group from Western Pioneer Life in Kentucky contacted me. Their offer seemed to be very fair and it protected everybody in the company, so I made a deal with them to help them buy the holding company for Ozark, I.C.H., Insurance Holding Company. I thought things were going to go smoothly now.

I was wrong.

One day a state insurance commissioner came to my office and announced that he was beginning an investigation into accusations of mismanagement of the company. The commission had received reports that I had secured the loans for the Texas real estate transaction with Ozark funds. I assured him that I had done nothing of the kind and I would be exonerated by his investigation. I wondered where he had heard a rumor like that, but I didn't have to wonder very long.

At our next regular board meeting, I walked in and sat down with the other ten board members. As I began the meeting, John Cantrell interrupted, "I have something I want to say."

I nodded to him. I thought he wanted to bring up some issue related to things on the agenda for the meeting. Instead, John looked around the room and said, "Charlie, we're going to vote on your position as president of Ozark National because of the insurance commission investigation."

I exploded, "If I've done something wrong, you won't have to fire me. I'll resign! But until you show me something I have done wrong, I'm not going to resign! I'm going to stay right here!"

John replied, "We'll vote on that."

I glared at him, "That's fine. Let's vote."

As people wrote down their votes, John just smiled. He knew he had me. I found out later that John had gone to the board members and enlisted the support of five of them to vote with him against me. He had convinced them I was guilty of the rumors and was unfit to lead the company. There were eleven board members, so these six constituted a majority. John left nothing to chance. He had them sign affidavits to be sure they would vote me down.

> As people wrote down their votes, John just smiled. He knew he had me.

When the votes were counted, however, there were six for me and five against me. One of the board members who had signed an affidavit, Charlie Duncan, had changed his mind. Duncan originally believed John, but between the time he signed the document and the day of the board meeting, he smelled a rat. So Charlie Duncan voted for me.

John's smirk turned to shock! He couldn't believe it! He stammered, "I demand a recount!"

I answered, "Okay, let's count them again."

We counted them again, and the results were the same: six for me and five against me.

During the recount, I quickly sized up the situation to figure out who was for me and who was against me. I leaned across the table and looked at my good friend and personal

Charlie and John Cantrell share a laugh at
a salesman trying on a cowboy hat

lawyer, Warren Donaldson, who was on the board. I told him, "Warren, you're fired!"

Some of the board members had a fit! They roared, "How can you do that to him?"

"It's easy! This man is a traitor!"

After a couple of minutes, Warren got up and walked out. An electrically charged meeting just went atomic!

I said, "Guys, I am going to tell you this. I'm still in the driver's seat. You may not like it, but that's the way it is. I promise you one thing: I'm going to straighten this thing out! If John Cantrell's lawyer can find something wrong that I've done, or if the insurance commission can find something wrong, I will resign. You won't have to vote on that . . . I'll just resign! That's a promise!"

After the board meeting, John took me aside and said, "Charlie, you did it again! I knew I had you, but you won." He paused for a second, then he asked, "Can we go up and pray in your office?"

I stared at him a few seconds to be sure he wasn't joking (I sure didn't think it was funny!), then I said, "Sure, John."

We walked up to my office and sat down. I told him, "I'll let you pray, but I'm going to watch because I'm afraid to close my eyes while you're in the room with me!"

John wanted to talk first. He explained the motivation behind his attempted coup. "I knew I had you, Charlie. I prayed about it. I just knew God was with me."

John was a deacon at his church. He was a spiritual leader, and he was convinced God had led him to deceive me and attempt to take over the company I had started. I had given him a good job with good pay, and he had repaid me by lying about me. Now he was trying to tell me that God was on his side.

I said, "John, I don't know how to be kind about this, but I can tell you one thing: God is certainly not with you in this lie! You need to open your eyes to that!" Our prayer meeting didn't last long. John prayed, but I kept my eye on him the entire time. This meeting wasn't about John's repentance. It was about his trying to get me to lower my guard. I wasn't going to play that game.

But John wasn't through playing games. He hired a lawyer and sued me for five million dollars for mismanaging Ozark National Life. I couldn't believe it! I assured John and his lawyer that those rumors were completely unfounded. I thought I had made my point very clearly. To find out the truth, Ozark hired the New York law firm of Wilke, Farr and Gallagher. (Presidential candidate Wendel Wilke was one of their original partners.)

> But John wasn't through playing games. He hired a lawyer and sued me for five million dollars for mismanaging Ozark National Life. I couldn't believe it!

About a week later, five attorneys from Wilke, Farr and Gallagher came to investigate. John's personal lawyer assisted them. Ozark National Life's offices had lawyers sitting on top of lawyers. Everybody had a lawyer: the company, John, and the insurance commission.

The company's New York lawyers wouldn't even look at me because they had been told lies about what I had done. This was a very painful time for me. I had been betrayed by two of my best friends in the world—one of them was a longtime friend I had brought into the insurance business, and the other was my lawyer. Now I was getting the cold shoulder from people whose sole purpose for being in our offices was to dig up dirt on me.

I tried to work things out with John. During the investigation, I told Bob Jackson, my new personal attorney, "Go see Clem Fairchild, Cantrell's attorney, and see if John and I can't sit down and talk. I want to see if we can straighten this thing out."

I invited John to my house, and he agreed to come. We sat down and I asked sincerely, "John, what in the world are you doing? You've known me for years, and you're telling people that I'm a crook. You know good and well that's not true. Why are you doing such a thing?"

John put his hand on my leg—I'll never forget that moment—and he told me, "Charlie, you are the most honest man I ever knew. You are honest to a fault."

I wanted to say, "Well, let's just drop this thing then!" But before I could answer, John said sternly, "This is the way to get you. And Charlie, I'm going to get you!"

I glared back at him, "John, don't hold your breath!"

He leaned forward and sneered, "I'm going to get you, Charlie! You can count on it."

Early one morning after about a week of investigation, one of the lawyers said "Good morning" as he walked past me. I thought this was odd. Soon, all the investigating law-yers began to talk to me. They became very pleasant and kind. Something dramatic had happened!

John Cantrell's attorney, Clem Fairchild, had turned over every rock in the company. I knew Clem very well, and if anything was there, he'd find it. But he didn't find a thing. The New York lawyers weren't finding anything in-criminating either, so I said, "Clem, how long are you go-ing to milk this thing? Why don't you just leave it alone

> John put his hand on my leg—I'll never forget that moment—and he told me, "Charlie, you are the most honest man I ever knew. You are honest to a fault."

and go on home because you know there's nothing here! You've got enough money out of it." He didn't respond, but I knew his game was over.

After another day or so, Clem told John, "I can't in good conscience proceed with the investigation and charge you any more money. It's just not worth it." John was so angry he fired Clem on the spot.

Clem Fairchild told my attorney, "We can't find any-thing wrong here."

The insurance department's attorney said, "I can't find anything wrong here."

The attorney hired by Ozark reported, "I can't find anything wrong here."

All of a sudden, the wheels fell off John Cantrell's wagon. I had been scrutinized under some of the best mi-croscopes in the legal world, and I was completely exonerated! (I couldn't believe they hadn't found *something* ! But they couldn't find a single instance of mismanagement. To be sure, I had made mistakes in judgment regarding my investments in the San Antonio apartments—and my mistakes had cost me a lot of money. But I never mingled my personal finances with the company's.) At long last, the insurance commission's lawyer and the swarm of New York lawyers went home.

Eventually, we bought John's stock and he left the company. If he had stayed, he could have made a fortune, but his desire for power was his undoing. I should have seen it coming when he suggested being president when we began the company.

Warren Donaldson and John Cantrell had orchestrated an elaborate conspiracy against me. Later, a man in the insurance commission told me Warren and John had started the rumors about my mishandling funds at Ozark. If they succeeded, Warren planned to take over as president and John would be the chairman of the board and Chief Executive Officer. But after the lawyers couldn't find anything to substantiate the accusations, they began to wonder why the charges had been leveled against me in the first place. All the fingers pointed back to John and Warren. Ultimately, the very people hired to investigate me uncovered the conspiracy.

Even in the midst of this problem, I sensed the hand of God at work. I wasn't bitter at God, and I wasn't even bitter at John Cantrell. Actually, I was amused at John and his games that backfired on him. It takes too much energy to be bitter, and there is no advantage in it. I never lifted even a little finger to hurt him in any way. I felt that the tension and heartache of being unfairly accused came because God was trying to get my attention. I had walked away from Him, and in His great love, He was getting my attention to call me back.

> I felt that the tension and heartache of being unfairly accused came because God was trying to get my attention.

I learned a very important lesson in all this: Don't try to get revenge. Just leave personal injustice alone, and God will take care of it. Paul wrote in Romans:

> Do not take revenge, my friends, but leave room
> for God's wrath, for it is written: "It is mine to
> avenge; I will repay," says the Lord.
> (Romans 12:19)

This passage doesn't say that the injustice doesn't matter. No, it says that it matters so much that God Himself is going to make it right! When we try to get even, we hurt ourselves by letting bitterness control us. We also get in the way of God's working in that person's life. We need to leave the situation and the person in God's strong hands. He is wise, and He is just. He can take care of that wound far better than we can.

I was confronted with a similar problem years later, and I had to remember the lesson of letting God have His way with those who try to hurt me. When I began to acquire land in northeast Missouri, some people in the community—and to be honest, some relatives of mine—accused me of all manner of heinous things. They told people I had a prostitution ring, I was selling drugs, and things like that. When asked why they were so angry at me, they would respond, "Just look at all he has! Only a pimp or a drug pusher has that much money!"

The thing that hurts is that none of those people took the time to talk to me, get to know me, or understand my heart and motives. I would do anything in the world to help them and be friends with them, but they never gave me the chance. Their jealousy, however, hurt them far more than it hurt me. In fact, the majority of those people have already died.

Bitterness kills.

Charlie and John Gehrke at an Ozark sales meeting, 1970

CHAPTER 5

ROCK BOTTOM . . . AND REBOUND

In spite of being completely exonerated by the investigation into my financial practices, my poor judgment on the real estate deal in Texas had eroded my credibility. I looked for a "white knight" to come in and help us so we could keep Ozark National. Bob Shaw and the people in Western Pioneer Insurance Company promised to help by merging their company with ours to help us through the current crisis. But in reality, they had no intention of doing what they said. The white knight soon turned into a slave master . . . and that slave was me!

At the time I had about three million dollars equity in my Ozark stock. I wasn't broke; I just didn't have the cash to service my debt. But as soon as the ink was dry on the agreement I signed with Western Pioneer, Bob Shaw (the new President and Chairman of the Board at Ozark) and the other new officers started orchestrating things so I would have to declare bankruptcy. They had promised to loan me enough money to service my debt in Texas, but they immediately backed away from their commitment because it wasn't in writing. It was a "gentlemen's agreement." The only problem was that they weren't gentlemen.

When they refused to loan me the money to pay the bank in Texas, I was forced to declare bankruptcy. It was not one of those Chapter 11 bankruptcies where the person comes out a millionaire. This was Chapter 7—the end, a financial disaster. I lost everything. In fact, I wound up owing the company $3,200,000! Instead of helping me get out of debt like they promised, they charged me for everything they could possibly think of. For instance, the wife of a friend who worked for Ozark died. He had been an important part of the company from the earliest years, so I wanted to attend his wife's funeral to show my support. I had used the company plane, so they charged me $4,000 for that trip.

A bankrupt person can't hold top management positions in an insurance company. When I had to step down as President and Chairman of the Board, I lost all my stock in Ozark and everything else of value. I remember sitting in my house waiting for the court-appointed movers to come take everything I owned. They came through like locusts, putting little tags on every piece of furniture, every pot and pan, and every picture on the wall. After they took it all out, all I had left were my clothes.

When I was a boy, I remember riding down the road with my dad. I saw a house and I asked, "Dad, who lives there?"

My dad said, "Oh, it doesn't matter. He didn't amount to anything."

That was all my dad said. I wondered what the story was with the man who lived there, but there was something in my dad's tone of voice that made me reluctant to ask another question. Later that day, we passed the same house. I said, "Dad, why did you say that man 'didn't amount to anything'?"

Dad replied simply, "He took bankruptcy, son."

> They came through like locusts, putting little tags on every piece of furniture, every pot and pan, and every picture on the wall. After they took it all out, all I had left were my clothes.

When I was a kid, there were two things you didn't do: You didn't get a divorce, and you didn't take bankruptcy. I had done both.

I sat on the floor in my empty house, and I pleaded, "Lord, let me die! I failed every way a man can fail! I've lost everything, and I've let my friends down. If it will help straighten the mess out, just let me die!"

Well, God didn't let me die that day. As a matter of fact, this was another important lesson for me in God's school of life. I realized I couldn't just sit and feel sorry for myself. I had to get up and get going again. I didn't have all the resources I had a few months ago, but I still had enough to make a fresh start. At this critical juncture, I came up with a phrase that has helped me gain perspective through many hard times: "Do all you can with what you've got, and you'll get some more."

I started selling insurance again, and those were the greatest years I ever had in my life. In fact, I stayed with Ozark as director of sales. Bob Shaw knew I was a skilled salesman, so he told me I could be a partner in the company. Some people have wondered why I would stay with a company that had treated me so badly. They ask if I was bitter toward them. No, I wasn't bitter. Bitterness never brings any positive changes. All my friends worked for the company, and I wanted to stay connected to them. I certainly wanted to stay in the insurance business, and I felt that Ozark was still the best place for me. I never talked badly about them to anyone. I just got up everyday and went to work.

From 1975 to 1980, I worked long and hard for Ozark, and I paid back the entire amount I owed them. At that point I felt like I should be reinstated to the leadership team. I had a sneaking suspicion, however, that the promises I had been given would be just as hollow this time as they had been in the beginning. I had seen far too much poor business practice and unscrupulous behavior by the corporate leaders. They made a boatload of promises they didn't keep. They were spending the company's money in frivolous ways. For example, they had spent over twenty million dollars on airplanes. Their investment management was terrible. They bought companies like Ozark, took all of the money out of

LINDA GENSLER

—Ozark Employee

People in this company are very loyal to Charlie because he is so consistent and so generous. He makes sure we have quarterly luncheons so he can talk to us and let us know what's going on. That's so important. He gives us wonderful Christmas bonuses, paid parking, and free lunches every day. Charlie finds neat ways to surprise us, like drawings from the Treasure Chest at Christmas where we get great things. Charlie makes working here fun and meaningful. He shows appreciation for our contribution to the company. He's terrific to work for.

As a policy service employee, I unfortunately had the responsibility of determining the cash value in Mr. Sharpe's personal life insurance policies when he went through bankruptcy. As the story goes: Not only did the pictures come off the walls and the dishes from the cupboard, they also took every penny from his life insurance policies. It was really sad. During that time, I'm sure he felt a lot of sorrow over what was going on. He didn't appear to be quite as positive and happy as I had known him to be. Most of us would be absolutely devastated; Mr. Sharpe only lost a little of his optimism.

Note: The four employees featured in this section have all been with Ozark National Life for many years, and all four have been honored as "Employee of the Year" for their outstanding contributions to the company.

DIANNA CARDELLO

—Ozark Employee

When I was a new employee, I loved working for Ozark. I remember telling my Dad, "I feel guilty taking my check." Well, not *that* guilty! Even during the bad times, I still had faith that Mr. Sharpe would come through somehow.

Later, Bob Shaw got control of our company and instituted a salary freeze for at least 18 months. This period was a low time for me—and for many others—in the company. It wasn't so much that we didn't get raises. It was more that the freeze made us feel the company wasn't as stable and our leadership wasn't as committed to us employees as before. That year Mr. Shaw refused to give any of us a Christmas bonus, so Charlie gave us one out of his own pocket. Charlie went from being president and founder to the director of the agency (in charge of the field agents who sold the policies). He is such a phenomenal salesman, and he thrived in that position—but then, he thrived, too, as president of the company.

LORRIE LASATER

—Ozark Employee

There was tremendous confusion when Mr. Shaw took over our company. One day Mr. Shaw walked into our data entry department and came to my desk. He asked me for the signature plate we used on checks. Of course, since he was the new president of the company, I gave it to him. He walked out of there with the signature plate, and in a few hours, we heard he was telling people, "There's no security at Ozark. I walked right in and got this signature plate with no problem at all. This is a big problem!" How was I going to tell the new president "No"? This experience told me a lot about Mr. Shaw.

We all loved and respected Mr. Sharpe, and the things we saw from Mr. Shaw discouraged and confused a lot of employees. One particular agent came in to the home office, and I remember complaining to him that things were going so badly. He told me, "Lorrie, Charlie will be back. You can count on that.

If you can hang on for a while through these bad times, Charlie will make it worth your while."

I always believed in Charlie, and that little pep talk really reassured me. When it comes down to it, we work for Charlie. We've always thought of it that way. Charlie *is* Ozark. Managers over us come and go—and we've gone through a lot of them—but Charlie is always here, and we're here for him. I've told him, "I don't know what I'm going to do when you're gone because I come to work every day for you."

HARRY
STAUFFER
—Ozark Employee

Even during the toughest times, Charlie was out motivating our agents and making the business go. Policyholders stayed with us, and we weathered the storm. Things here at the home office were in a turmoil under Mr. Shaw's leadership. There were accusations and snap decisions. A lot of good people here left the company. At one point, we lost some programmers when Mr. Shaw shipped our computer to Dallas for some reason. They came in and took our tapes and our mainframe. We were still responsible for printing, but we didn't have the computer anymore. That was a slap in our faces. But later, Charlie was able to take over again, and we returned to normal operations.

My highest moments at Ozark National Life were when I received my 10th year anniversary diamond ring and when we had the company's 30th year celebration. Both of those symbolized stability and success.

those companies that they could possibly take out, and used that money to buy additional companies. The practice wasn't actually illegal, but it certainly wasn't good for the companies being bought. I was in the hands of incompetent, unethical, unscrupulous people.

As I anticipated my conversation with the leadership, I wanted to believe the best—but I feared the worst. I called Bob Shaw and said, "Bob, I want to see you. Would you come over to my house?"

Bob responded, "Sure, Charlie. I'll be right over."

We lived close to each other, so it only took him a few minutes to arrive. He came in and sat down. I said, "Bob, I've asked you this five or six times, and I never get a straight answer. I'm going to ask you again. Am I a partner in the company or not?"

He smiled and rolled his head back and forth a bit like people do when their words don't match their thoughts. "Well, Charlie, *of course* you are a partner." He paused, then he continued, "But you know very well you're not a partner *on paper*."

I said, "Now wait a minute, Bob. If I'm a partner, I'm a partner all the way."

He laughed at my naiveté, "No, Charlie, we can't do that."

I said, "If I'm not a partner in the company, I've been lied to, I've been taken advantage of, I've been abused, and I'm not going to take it anymore. I am here to tell you that I am leaving the company!"

Bob said, "What are you going to do?"

I said, "I started *this* company. I'll start another one!" I had purchased an option on an insurance company in Pennsylvania to show Bob that I was dead serious about leaving and starting another company.

He said, "You can't do that. You're bankrupt! You've lost everything! Who would follow you?"

I said, "Well, let's find out!"

I set up meetings with Ozark salespeople all over the country to tell them about my plans to start a new company. These were people who had worked with me for years. I had hired most of them. I didn't ask them to leave Ozark and join me. I only wanted to tell them my plans and see if they wanted to come along. If they did, fine. If not, that would be fine, too. If they chose to come with me, it would be a huge risk for them, but a company that lies to its employees isn't worthy of the loyalty of its people. After these meetings, I had 437 signed affidavits of salespeople who would leave the company and go with me!

I brought the stack of affidavits back to the corporate office and plopped them down on Bob Shaw's desk. He looked through the stack as I stood watching him, then he looked up at me and said, "I can't believe it! There's not that many fools in the world!"

I said, "There must be. These are their signatures!"

He was going to lose the most valuable people in the company, so he found a way out. "Maybe we'd better sell you the company, Charlie."

I said, "I think you should."

Bob asked, "How are you going to pay for it? You have no money."

I responded confidently, "You are going to finance it."

Sixteen men, the top managers in Ozark, stood with me to buy Ozark from Western Pioneer. These men put up everything they owned as collateral. I was bluntly honest with them: "Fellas, if you go with me, you could lose everything! You could lose every dime of your commissions! I wouldn't blame you one bit if you said 'No.' " One of the men, Gene Montee, went home and talked to his wife Marjorie about it. They had been married for years, and Gene had bought Marge a large diamond ring just a few weeks before the insurance commission investigation blew sky high. It was a ring she had dreamed of wearing. As Gene and Marge discussed the company's predicament and our need for cash to buy out Bob Shaw, Gene asked, "Are we going with Charlie, or are we going to stay where we are? The choice, Marge, is between loyalty and safety." Without a word, Marge pulled the ring off her finger, gave it to Gene, and said, "Gene, we're going with Charlie. If we have to sell the ring to help Charlie make it, we'll sell the ring."

> Sixteen men, the top managers in Ozark, stood with me to buy Ozark from Western Pioneer. These men put up everything they owned as collateral.

I'll never forget that.

We formed a new holding company, National Insurance Services, and Western Pioneer financed 100 percent of our purchase of Ozark with an interest rate we could afford. This was another example of the mercy of God to work even when we didn't see His gracious hand. God enabled us to rescue Ozark—and the jobs of hundreds of employees—from certain oblivion if Bob Shaw and his people had remained in control. Only a few years later, Shaw's holding company collapsed; its stock is worthless.

We signed the agreement to buy the company in 1981, and from that day on we got up every day and went to work to rebuild and protect the company. God brought about His justice for me that day, and He restored the years the locust had eaten. Bob Shaw couldn't take any more money out of the company. He had to leave it alone. Ozark grew and became a very healthy company during the next few years.

Every year we reduced the loan we had gotten to buy the company. I was the president, but until the loan was paid off, I didn't have control of the company. Ozark grew stronger for several years. Our profits were up, and sales-people were doing a fantastic job. Company morale was as high as it had ever been.

Then, in 1986, the lid blew off again. The state insur-ance commission informed me that accusations had been levied against me and my leadership of the company. (As Yogi Berra would say, "It was deja vu all over again!")

This news hit me like a punch in the stomach. I had started this company; I had built it up, lost control of it, and watched other people almost destroy it. I had taken over again and built it into a strong, sound company with loyal, dedicated people. Now I was being accused again of mismanagement.

As the investigation began, I seriously questioned my own integrity. After all, I reasoned, "Where there's smoke there's fire." And there was plenty of smoke! Surely, I thought, I must have done some really awful things . . . but even worse, I'm not smart enough to even know I've done them! I have not often been plagued with self-doubt, but this was a dark period for me.

But in that darkness, I sought the Lord more than I had sought Him in years. I read the Bible, and I prayed, "Lord, it sure looks like You want to get my attention. Show me, God. Show me Your will." I still hadn't recommitted my life to Christ, but I was at least aware of His presence and power, and I was honestly seeking His wisdom.

As the investigation began, I realized the accusations were vague. Nothing specific was stated. That was a red flag. I asked questions of the commission, and they told me that an anonymous person had repeatedly told them, "We know things about Charlie Sharpe that disqualify him from securing control of Ozark National." Now, as the loan was about to be paid off, the accusations came to the commission like machine gun fire! At first, the commission had ignored the allegations, but as they intensified, they decided to investigate.

Who was behind all this? Bob Shaw.

He never had any intention of letting Ozark National get away from him. His scheme was to let me own the company, build it back up, then conspire to destroy my character so he could step in and take over again.

Bob Shaw

Just as I had done years earlier, I chose to fight the accusations with the truth. I told my people and the investigator, "We are going to bring everything out into the open. If I've done something wrong, all of us are going to know about it! There won't be any questions left unanswered. There won't be any vague accusations. The truth will be plain."

I hired a terrific lawyer, John "Woody" Cozad, who soon became a great friend. I told him, "Woody, I want to get control of my company, and I want to go for broke! I can't stand these innuendoes any longer. Either I will control Ozark or Bob Shaw will, but we can't go on like this any more."

Woody subpoenaed Bob Shaw. On the day of his deposition, Bob came with his lawyer (who, incidentally, was the lawyer I used when I formed the company back in 1964). Woody and I walked in together, and the state insurance commissioner attended the deposition, too.

Under oath, Bob was asked what he knew about my alleged mismanagement that made me unfit to run an insurance company. For several minutes, Bob hemmed and hawed. It was obvious that he couldn't produce one shred of evidence. His entire ploy had been a bluff. I felt great! I was vindicated! Then I looked over at the insurance commissioner. He was so angry he was beet red! He was furious! Bob Shaw had lied to him, manipulated him, and wasted his time.

At the end of the deposition, Woody and I announced to the commissioner that we were going to file for complete control of Ozark. The commissioner was, shall we say, fairly receptive to us! To get control, we had to complete the payoff of the loan to Shaw's company.

On the day we appeared before the insurance commission to appeal for our certificate and control of the company, I took seventeen people who stood with me. In the hearing room, they listened to the commissioner announce, "We see no reason why Charles Sharpe cannot control this company." At that moment, all of us cheered! Ozark was finally free from Bob Shaw. It was a happy day!

The lesson for all of us is: Just hang in there, and don't quit! The only person who loses is the one who quits. I gave the people 40 percent of the company, and when I paid them out ten years later, they received a total of forty-six million dollars.

Another lesson here is the power of the people. The Lord showed me in all of this that He frequently acts through people. How did God free the children of Israel from slavery in Egypt? He used Moses. How did He conquer the Promised Land? He used Joshua, Caleb, and others. What was God's plan to spread the gospel after Christ ascended? He used the disciples, and then all the new believers. Throughout the Old and New Testaments, in story after story, God used people to accomplish His purposes. Sometimes people understood God's plan and followed it to fulfill His designs, but sometimes they were completely unaware that God's strong hand was behind their decisions and their actions. And God used the people of Ozark to accomplish His purposes of getting us free from Bob Shaw.

Before all this trouble started, Bob and I had discussed our different ways of doing business. I said, "Bob, if we ever come to the parting of the ways for any reason, you take the money and give me the people. And it won't be very long till I have the money back." That's exactly the way it turned out. To be sure, Bob tried to take the money *and* the people, but the people chose to go with me. My comments to Bob that day were prophetic, and I didn't even know it.

Loyalty is built on years of integrity in the give-and-take of life and business. When people see that your word is good time after time, they learn to trust you. This kind of relationship can't be built overnight, and it can't be demanded. It is earned. And loyalty isn't based on being perfect, either. If it were, I'd be in big trouble. But trust is also built when a person is willing to say those rare words, "I was wrong." Honesty and a touch of humility go a long way in building relationships in which people feel comfortable, and they are motivated to do their very best because they feel loved and honored as human beings. These seventeen people, along with many other agents at Ozark, saw that I wouldn't sell

> Honesty and a touch of humility go a long way in building relationships in which people feel comfortable, and they are motivated to do their very best because they feel loved and honored as human beings.

out to Bob Shaw. They knew I was here—no matter what—because they had seen me stick it out through the darkest days we had ever experienced. They stated, "Charlie, whatever the situation is, we think that we would be better off with you than without you."

How important is loyalty to people? I will tell you this: Without loyalty, you have no life! Trustworthy relationships produce the willingness to sacrifice for others. These relationships are the glue that holds people together through thick and thin. The reason we're in such terrible shape in our society today is because people aren't loyal. Instead of loyalty to someone or something else, they want to know: "What's in this for me?"

Ozark looked very strong at this point when we took control of the company, and several of the original investors chose this time to cash out. The first investor, Dr. Kapp, the dentist who invested during a root canal, sold his stock and made fifteen million dollars. Some investors stayed with Bob Shaw's holding company after we gained control of Ozark in 1986. One of those was Charlie Duncan, the board member who had signed the affidavit for John Cantrell to fire me but changed his mind. Duncan, and every other stockholder in Shaw's holding company, lost everything they had. At one time, Shaw's holding company had over nine billion dollars in assets. Today, the company is defunct.

Loyalty to a bad cause will destroy you. Charlie Duncan lost several million dollars. Loyalty, in and of itself, is not the most important thing. It's who you are loyal to that really counts. You've got to be loyal to the right cause.

HUGH WYATT

—33 years with Ozark National Life, Assistant to the President from 1974 to 1976

Through a mutual friend named Eldon Morgan, Charlie contacted me in New Orleans in July of 1966 because he wanted to start operations in Louisiana. He was looking for six men to be on the board of his company in our state, and he met with me to see if I was interested in being one of those men. Eldon knew I had just sold two restaurants, and he thought Charlie might have a good opportunity for me.

When I met with Charlie, he told me he already had the money he needed to start business in Louisiana. He was looking for men who had a good reputation and a proven character to serve on the board. We talked for about an hour, and in that short time, I was thoroughly convinced that Charlie Sharpe was a man of integrity and vision. Though he didn't need any money, he offered to let me buy an interest in the company. We had just come through Hurricane Betsy, and I had spent some of the money from the sale of the restaurants on home repairs. I had about $10,500 left, and that's what I intended to invest. When I did the math in my head, however, I got a little confused. The number of shares I told him I wanted to buy was only $1500 worth. When Charlie mentioned the figure of $1500, I realized my math was wrong. I said, "Charlie, I didn't mean to say $1500. I meant to say $10,500."

Charlie told me, "I'll have to go to some others and ask them to give up some of their shares, and I'll give up some of mine. But if that's what it takes to have you with us, that's what we'll do."

It meant a lot to me that Charlie wanted me personally more than my money. He was just as happy (and maybe even happier) with me putting in $1500 as he was with me putting in $10,500. The money wasn't the issue to him. That told me a lot about his integrity.

After we agreed on our arrangement, Charlie asked me if I knew of an office nearby where we could get an agreement typed up for us to sign. He told me that he had not yet finalized the acquisition of an existing company which would become Ozark National of Louisiana, so I'd have to make out a check to him personally. "Of course, I'll give you a receipt," he told me plainly.

I called a friend, James Ganus, and asked if we could use his office to draft an agreement, and he said "Yes." Charlie and I got into a cab and drove to downtown New Orleans. In the office, my friend assigned one of his secretaries to type the agreement as Charlie dictated it. It read simply, "I, Charles N. Sharpe, receive from Hugh A. Wyatt the sum of $10,500, which is to be converted to stock in what is to become Ozark National Life of Louisiana." Before the secretary finished, she asked to be excused. Charlie nodded. She went into the office of her boss—and my friend whose office we were using—to tell him about the transaction. While Charlie sat patiently next to the secretary's vacant desk, James called me into his office and asked me, "Hugh, do you know what you're doing?"

I replied, "Yes, James. I'm going to be on the board of an insurance company."

James nodded toward a huge safe in his office. "Hugh, I could open that safe and take out enough worthless stock certificates from insurance companies to paper the walls of this office. How long have you known this man you're doing business with?"

"About an hour."

He winced, "Hugh, are you sure you know what you're doing?"

I told him, "James, the man who recommended Mr. Sharpe to me I hold in the same esteem as I hold you. I believe Mr. Sharpe is a man of integrity and can be trusted."

James nodded affirmingly, and I walked back to Charlie and completed our transaction. That was the beginning of a long and pleasant relationship with Charlie Sharpe.

A few years later, the business was doing well and stock was trading at about $40. Not many shares were being traded, and I wanted to buy 100 shares. On a particular day, two blocks of stock became available to Charlie, but one of the blocks was priced a little higher than the other. He offered me one of the blocks of stock, and I found out later from one of the secretaries (who are the sources of all truth in any company!) that Charlie had offered me the one priced lower while he bought the other one. His decision saved me a few dollars and cost him those dollars. I would never have known, and he would never have told me, but this, too, is another example of his integrity. The secretary's disclosure was just one more evidence that Charlie would never take advantage of anyone.

When Bob Shaw and Fred Rice of Western Pioneer took over Ozark, they attended sales meetings all over the country and made promises that Charlie would eventually have equal ownership with them in the parent corporation and that Charlie eventually would be reinstated as president of Ozark. The more we knew about Shaw and Rice, the more we looked forward to having Charlie back in charge. It gradually became obvious to all of us that Shaw and

Rice were not committed to us as people or as employees. The differences between their leadership style and Charlie's could not have been more pronounced. After those initial trips to introduce themselves and make promises about the future, Shaw and Rice seldom attended sales meetings; Charlie was always there. Shaw and Rice were motivated for profits; Charlie motivated each of us to do and be our best. Shaw and Rice were distant and aloof; Charlie was (and is) always available to listen and encourage people.

Some time later, Shaw announced in a meeting in Orlando, Florida, that it was time for Charlie to be reinstated as the president. We looked forward to having our leader back at the helm of the company. However, in only a short time, Charlie noticed that Shaw and Rice were hedging on that commitment. Charlie asked them several times to clarify his position, but every time, they made promises which they didn't act on.

Soon the handwriting was on the wall: Shaw and Rice were not going to live up to their commitments to Charlie. Equal ownership of the parent company with Shaw and Rice and control of the agency force were the only ways to control the destiny of Ozark. We all knew that from the beginning. Soon after we realized Shaw and Rice were not honoring their word, five of us attended a meeting in Kansas City with Charlie, Shaw, and Rice. These five were Janet Fairchild, who was head of the fund brokerage, Roy Elsworth, who ran the agency, and the three regional managers: Melvin Roewe, Byron Wood, and me. We asked for this meeting in order to convince Shaw and Rice to live up to their commitment to the sales force and to Charlie. We demanded that they reinstate Charlie as the president of Ozark and assign the appropriate share of ownership to him.

The meeting lasted all day, but at the end, Shaw and Rice refused to comply with their clear, stated commitments. In the early evening, Charlie resigned and walked out. He said, "That's it! I refuse to go any further with unscrupulous people."

After Charlie left the room, Bob Shaw looked at Melvin, Byron, and me and said, "I didn't want Charlie to resign, but it's done now. The company must go on. I want one of you three to become the president of the company. The one who accepts the position will have a salary of $250,000 a year. You'll have an unlimited expense account and use of the Lear jet. Let me know which of you will take the job." His plan was that one of us would be enticed by that offer to turn his back on Charlie, each other . . . and our honor.

The night passed, but none of the three of us took the bait. Rice and Shaw then had to figure out how to run the company without a president. That next morning, Fred Rice took us to the agency department in Ozark and assigned the three of us to oversee each aspect of the entire operations. We became, in effect, a three-headed president by default.

Shaw knew that if Charlie left and Melvin, Byron, and I were unwilling to unite the agency force, virtually every manager and every agent would leave Ozark, leaving it barren of sales and with no hope of profit and service. Shaw also knew that Charlie had already obtained an option on another insurance company, and he planned to hire all of us to work with him if the negotiations with Shaw broke down. Our plan was to leave in waves: agents first, then district managers, then zone managers, then regional managers, and then Charlie would leave the company. But that plan was accelerated when Charlie resigned.

Charlie came in that morning to clear out his desk and move out of his office. Bob Shaw realized he had been beaten by our unity, so he called Charlie and met with him. He agreed to sell the company back to Charlie. That moment was one of the most significant turning points in the history of Ozark National Life. The courage and unity of every person in the company was galvanized because of the loyalty we all felt toward Charlie. If one of the top managers had faltered, the history of the company—and of each person involved—would be very different. But none of us wavered, even in the face of grand promises, promotions, or threats. We stayed rock-solid behind the one we believed in.

It is sad to look back and realize that Shaw and Rice ultimately lost everything when their own company's value plummeted. If they had kept their word, they could have had an incredible leader in Charlie and a solid, effective sales force in the rest of us. But they chose to turn their backs on honor and integrity.

Over the years, I've noticed that Charlie is incredibly observant about people. In even short conversations, he picks up on things that give him a green light to do business with someone or a red flag of caution. This ability has served him—and us—very well to keep us away from people who said the right things but who had hidden agendas the rest of us didn't notice. When he got a green light with someone, he is the best motivator I've ever known in my life. He believed in us, and he challenged us to do our best. And he never gave up on us no matter what.

There are very few companies which provide genuine access to the top executive, but at Ozark National Life, Charlie is open and available to every single person in the company. He has proven over and over again that he cares about each of us. I've known a lot of people in my sixty-nine years, but I've never known a man as unselfish as Charlie Sharpe. We all value fairness, but Charlie consistently goes far beyond fair. He makes sure that people are treated well—surprisingly well. He knows how to have fun and laugh, but much more than that, he knows how to care. Charlie makes sure all our sales meetings are as wholesome as they can possibly be. There is never anything off color or offensive. Charlie treats us like his own family. Nothing ever happens at a sales meeting that you wouldn't feel comfortable bringing your wife or your mother to see.

Our ability to offer the balanced program of insurance and mutual funds has given us a very valuable product to offer our clients. Those of us who have been in the company for a while can point to hundreds of people who have literally become millionaires because of the genius of this balanced program. For example, I think of one couple, an ordinary working couple, who began a forty-five dollar a month program with us in 1969. Today, their mutual fund account is over two-and-a-half million dollars. We've helped our clients accumulate over two billion dollars in mutual funds.

Like our other sales people, I am motivated by many things, but the deepest motivation is to help people reach their goals and fulfill their dreams. Ozark National Life has helped me do that for people. I could be retired right now, but as long as I am mentally capable, I want to keep helping people through Ozark National Life. That desire is the direct result of Charlie's vision and enthusiasm, our terrific products, and the look in people's eyes when they realize how much we've helped them. Today, I have many clients who call me and recommend one of their friends to me who want help with insurance or investments. Our satisfied clients tell their friends about us. That's the best compliment we could ever receive.

GENE MONTEE

—Former Ozark Vice President, retired, 35 years with the company

Ozark National began operations in April of 1964, and in June, Charlie contacted me about working for him. I was a sales trainer for another insurance company, Farmer's. A man I had trained told Charlie about me, so Charlie called me and asked me head up the company's new operations in Kansas. At the time, I had been in the insurance business for fifteen years, and I had read several books about the impact of inspirational leaders in this business, so I had a good feel for what it takes to be an entrepreneur, a motivator who can inspire others to excel. As soon as I met Charlie, I could tell he was one of those rare people who could do what I'd been reading about. It was as clear as a bolt of lightning. I knew a winner when I saw one.

I had been approached by many other companies in those fifteen years. They had promised me all kinds of things if I'd go with them, but here was a man who promised me nothing but opportunity. I went home and talked to my wife Marjorie. She was eager to hear about my meeting with Charlie. I explained to her that I was impressed with his enthusiasm and his vision. He was a man I could follow because I saw a true greatness in him. She asked me, "Are you going to work for him, Gene?"

I told her, "I think so."

Her wheels started turning: "Are you going to be a manager?"

"No."

"Will you have a salary?"

"No."

"Will you get a bonus?"

"No."

"Will you get a company car?"

"No."

By this time, she was getting a little nervous! She continued to ply me with questions. "What's the name of this man's company?"

"He hasn't decided on a name yet."

Well, if you want to inspire a woman who has two hungry kids to feed, this wasn't the way to do it!

I explained that Charlie had asked me to start over at the bottom of the company and learn his way of doing things from the ground up. I could tell she wasn't too sure about all this, but she knew my mind was made up. I left one of the oldest and most stable insurance companies in the country, and started at the bottom of a brand new company. My friends at Farmer's told me I was crazy to make the change. I was making good money, I had a good job, and I played golf twice a week. What more could you want in life? They couldn't understand why I would leave that security to work for Charlie Sharpe. But they hadn't met him. I had.

Charlie told me that I could stay at that level of a district manager and trainer at Farmer's all my life, but if I went with him, he'd challenge me to reach my full potential. Charlie never gave promises, only challenges. I liked that. To be honest, there was one promise Charlie made to me. He told me, "If you'll go with me, you'll find out how good you can be." I could do the job at Farmer's standing on my head. It had become easy because I had reached, as Charlie calls it, my "comfort level." But at Ozark, I started at the bottom and held every position all the way up from agent to Vice President, and at one point, I was on his Board of Directors.

Charlie wasn't the kind to give lavish verbal praise if you did well. He was afraid that if you got too much praise you'd let up and stop pushing yourself. He made sure you set the bar a little higher after every success. He rewards success more than anyone I've ever known, but he doesn't want you to quit reaching, pushing, and achieving more, so he

keeps raising the bar for you. I have never seen anyone motivate people as much as Charlie does. He
believes in people, and they know it . . . they feel it,
and they begin to believe in themselves, too. That's
a powerful impact on people. There were many times
over the years that I was mad at him for pushing
me, but if he hadn't believed in me so much, I'd still
be a district manager at Farmer's.

One of the things I always appreciated about
Charlie was that he was himself in every situation.
He never changed. I remember one time we had a
meeting in Wichita of over 1,000 sales people.
Charlie's presentation to them was incredibly enthusiastic and positive, but it was no different than
another sales meeting I recall a few years before
when there were only fifteen or twenty of us who
attended: the same enthusiasm, the same vision, the
same Charlie. I believe that's the essence of integrity: to be consistently yourself in every situation.
But Charlie didn't say the same thing every time he
spoke. He always had a fresh insight and a new story
to illustrate his points. Nobody ever got tired of listening to the man.

I remember the dark days of the company when
another company bought Ozark and took control.
Promises were made to Charlie and to the rest of us.
These promises, however, weren't kept, so Charlie
resigned. Many of us in the company decided we
couldn't stay if Charlie left. I was about 55 years old

at that time, and I sure didn't want to start over somewhere else. I wanted him to take over Ozark. We met with Charlie, and we formulated a plan to buy the company from Shaw. Sixteen of us who were officers in Ozark signed notes totaling $37.5 million. Each of us put up all of our personal belongings as collateral. Marjorie and I put up our house, our cars, the commissions I would earn in the next five years, and every other asset we owned. If we bought the company and it failed, we would have lost literally everything we owned in this world. At my age at the time, that was not a pleasant prospect. People have wondered why in the world the sixteen of us were willing to stake everything on Charlie and Ozark, but the answer is very simple: We believed in Charlie Sharpe. We had complete confidence that Charlie would make it work, and to my knowledge, not one of us ever had second thoughts about going out on that limb with him.

Marjorie always thought Charlie Sharpe was just about the best thing that ever came into our lives. Charlie is a fantastic leader, and both of us—Marjorie and I—knew we wanted to hitch our wagon to that horse. Charlie made sure he communicated very clearly to our wives as well as to us sixteen, so he took time to explain the risks and the benefits of the buy-out to Marjorie. She listened carefully, then she told him, "Charlie, we're with you. If I have to hock my diamond rings, I'll do it." That meant a lot to Charlie for Marjorie to be so much behind him.

Charlie feels just as comfortable in blue jeans talking to working men as he does having lunch with bank presidents. He has the unique ability to fit in perfectly with anybody anytime in any situation. But Charlie feels most at home with Ozark employees. His enthusiasm is infectious. I remember the first time Marjorie and I went to an Ozark agents' meeting. We almost turned and ran out the door because they were giving "the Ozark yell": "Give me an O! Give me a Z! Give me. . . ." I had worked for a dignified, established, national insurance company where the president was so formal he turned off the microphone if he wanted to clear his throat. Now I was watching the president of Ozark lead his people in the Ozark yell, and all the employees were standing and yelling with all their hearts! All insurance companies have to have good products and good principles, but Ozark added the element of enthusiasm. That makes a world of difference!

One of the things I always appreciated about Charlie is that he gives people a second and third chance. In any company as big as Ozark, employees come and go. Sometimes people who leave say all kinds of terrible things about their bosses. A few of these people said awful things about Charlie, but if they came back, he forgave them and welcomed them back into the company. That's happened many times over the years. I don't think I could forgive some of these people if they had treated me that way, but Charlie forgave them and gave them another chance. It's easy to follow a great leader like him.

RICHARD LUELF

—Began working for Ozark when he was 23 years old, Vice President from 1989 to 1991

When I was an agent with Ozark in 1967, a district manager put up billboards all over the state of Missouri that read: "Ozark National Life—The company that's different." I was traveling around the state selling insurance, and I stopped in Union, Missouri, and met a district manager for Midwest National Life Insurance. (Paul Jones, the president of Midwest National Life, was the brother of Pat Jones, who was the president of Modern Security where Charlie worked before he started Ozark.) Midwest's district manager knew that Ozark salesmen worked out of their cars. He looked down his nose at me and said, "We have offices. That means stability."

I looked him right in the eye and said, "Yeah, but we have Charlie Sharpe."

He laughed, "Well, you'll see what happens down the road. Your billboard says you're 'different.' You'll see who's left standing."

We turned out to be a lot different than Midwest National Life Insurance Company. A few years later, Ozark was going strong, and Midwest National Life was out of business.

Charlie was the best thing that ever happened to agents in the field. He spoke at every event we could schedule to tell people about our products, and he went out in the field with agents to show them how to better help customers. Charlie has never been an "ivory tower" executive who observes from a distance. He rolls up his sleeves and gets out there with the agents.

I was made a district manager in 1967 when I was twenty-six years old, and for three years in a row we had the top district in the company. At that time, Charlie announced Ozark was going to start up operations in Texas, and he asked four men to go there to head up that new operation. I wondered why he didn't ask me to go, and I talked to Charlie about it. I expected to be promoted since my district had been the top in the company for three years in a row. Charlie told me, "Rich, you're kind of young to be promoted again so soon."

I told him, "If you let me go to Texas, I'll show you what I can do!"

He agreed to let me go, but I'd have to start over as an agent. I told him that was fine with me. I was glad to have the opportunity. The other men arrived in Texas a few months before I did, but I reached my goal of being the first agent in Texas to write $1 million in new policies. The challenge of proving myself to Charlie was a big motivator for me, and I rose to the challenge.

Charlie could have told me I couldn't go to Texas, but he saw the determination in my eye and he encouraged me to go for my dreams. Many times over the years, Charlie met with me and encouraged me to dream bigger and reach farther. He believed in me more than anybody in the world ever has, and I love him for it.

Years later, after Bob Shaw got control of the company and failed to fulfill his promises to Charlie, many of us in the company realized we couldn't stay connected to Shaw and his people. It was simply too much of a risk to work for someone like that unless Charlie was on board and leading our group of agents. Charlie tried to buy Ozark, but Shaw refused to sell to him. At that point, Charlie wanted to show Shaw that he meant business, so he put $100,000 of his own money down as an option to buy an insurance company in Pennsylvania. Shaw was glad to see Charlie go, but he wasn't prepared for what happened next. Mr. Shaw called three or four of Ozark's top managers to a meeting in

Kansas City and individually offered them an opportunity to stay with Ozark, lead the sales force, and replace Charlie. One after the other, they each told Shaw, "If Charlie goes, I go." At that point, Shaw realized that if Charlie left, he'd lose all the Ozark staff. And if all of us left, we'd take all our business with us and gut the company.

In the heat of this power struggle, Ozark had a sales convention in Wichita, Kansas. One night, Charlie invited sixteen of his top field managers to go to a secret meeting with him in a room at another hotel in the city. We had a guard stationed at the door to protect us in case Shaw got wind of our secret meeting. That's how tense things were! In that meeting, Charlie told us about his plan for us to help him buy the company. At that time, he had just gone through personal bankruptcy, so each of the sixteen of us had more to lose than he did. But that didn't matter. We were glad he wanted us to join him.

Even though I was younger than some of the men who put up everything to back Charlie in buying Ozark from Bob Shaw, I was proud to be counted as one of them. I had seen Charlie lead the company and motivate people so incredibly well that I had total confidence in him. One of Shaw's vice presidents once said about me, "If Charlie Sharpe asked Richard Luelf to walk on water, Richard would do it." He meant that as a slam against me, but I took it as a compliment. In fact, I felt all sixteen of us were ridiculed by Shaw's people for risking every dime we had in going with Charlie, but we believed it was far more of a risk to trust someone like Bob Shaw than it was to trust a proven leader like Charlie.

Over the years, I've had plenty of offers to work for other companies. They think they are offering me a great opportunity to work for them, but they have no idea how strongly I feel about Charlie and Ozark. Charlie is a terrific businessman, but he is also the most caring person I've ever known. People around him know that he genuinely cares about them. Years ago I went through a divorce, and Charlie helped me through that difficult time in my life. At another time, our house burned, and Charlie called me immediately to offer his help. Yes, he's built a big business and his career is based on lots of great business principles, but if you ask me what characterizes the man most of all, it's that he cares.

Ozark National Life Building, acquired 1985

Lobby

Charlie and Laurie, 1987

CHAPTER 6

A NEW LOVE

In 1980, my secretary at Ozark got engaged. She and her fiancé planned to move to another city, so she would be leaving Ozark. She knew I would be interviewing women to take her place, so she volunteered, "My roommate might be able to do this job for you."

I needed to start looking for a replacement right away, so I told her, "Why don't you have her come in?"

A few days later, Laurie Emerson showed up for an interview. I knew immediately that she did not have the skills to do the job, but I could tell she was a fine young woman. In our first conversation, I could see a strong sense of loyalty in her character. She was a bright girl, but keeping up with me is an awesome responsibility—especially since we were in the middle of buying Ozark National from Bob Shaw.

I decided to hire her and train her so she could acquire the skills she needed. I believe character is more important than skills. Skills can be learned fairly easily; character can't. On Laurie's first day, I was sure she wasn't going to make it. She got behind from the moment she walked in, and during the day, she got buried even deeper in all the calls, schedules, and details. When I walked out the door that evening, I had serious doubts that Laurie would work out as my secretary. But the next morning, I walked in, looked at her desk, and I saw that she had all her work done. She had caught up! This scenario occurred day after day. The only way for her to catch up was to work most of the night. I was constantly amazed at her dedication to complete her tasks at night after I was gone, and she never complained about the work load and the hours. I knew from early on that she was a person of proven character.

> On Laurie's first day, I was sure she wasn't going to make it.

Laurie wasn't very talkative at all. In fact, she was sometimes painfully timid. I knew this was a skill she could acquire, and I wanted to help her. That's an easy task for me! I just talked to her—all day every day.

After several months, I decided to take Laurie to dinner. She worked until 8, 9, or 10 o'clock every night. We were both single, but we observed that we certainly didn't need to be concerned about our having any kind of relationship. I was an old man, and Laurie was in her early 20s. Our dinners together were more for convenience than anything else, but we enjoyed being together.

I asked Laurie to attend sales meetings with me so she could meet our field people and learn the business a little better. She had talked to all those people on the phone many times, so it was good for her to meet them face to face. The dinners . . . the travel . . . and almost continual interactions at the office began to form a bond between us that neither of us expected. After about a year, we both realized that our relationship of convenience had become genuine affection. We were dating!

It seemed so ridiculous! I think Laurie had an early interest in me, and of course, I was certainly attracted to her. It bothered me tremendously, however, because she was so young, and I never would have gotten into a position where I was taking advantage of her in any way, shape, or form.

Even if I had wanted to take advantage of her, Laurie wouldn't allow that. She is extremely independent. If there ever was a person who can think for herself, it's Laurie. She wasn't dependent on me in the least. To be honest, that's one of the things that attracted me to her. Sometimes people misinterpret her quietness as weakness, but she has the heart of a lion.

As the relationship grew over the next couple of years, I often felt terribly awkward. I tried to talk her out of it. On several occasions, I said, "Laurie, you know this can't be. We just can't do this!" She was used to my making decisions at the office, so she wondered if this was one of my cut-and-dried conclusions. She was hurt and confused, and I was probably the most miserable human being in the world. I realized how much a part of me she had become,

> As the relationship grew over the next couple of years, I often felt terribly awkward. I tried to talk her out of it.

and I certainly didn't want to lose her. I think she felt the same way about me. We had a host of starts and stops, red lights and green lights. Both of us enjoyed the relationship, but both of us saw how ludicrous it was for us to be dating. We'd heard of May-September relationships; this was more like February-November!

The shy, quiet girl who was my secretary developed remarkable skills and maturity. After several years of working with me, an opportunity opened for Laurie. As Ozark had grown, she and I had handled the organizational needs of the salespeople around the country. There were so many of them now, however, we just couldn't keep up. We decided to form a new department to service these agents, and we began looking for the right person to head that department. Soon it became apparent that Laurie had the skills, the savvy, and the experience to do the job very well, so we promoted her and she thrived in that role. We didn't see each other quite as much every day, but our relationship continued to grow and develop.

Our relationship continued for several years, and I felt it was hindering Laurie from pursuing younger men and having a more normal life. At dinner one night in 1989, I made a final determination and announced, "Laurie, this is wrong. We need to stop seeing each other."

I don't know who was more heartbroken, Laurie or me. The decision crushed us. We were both miserable. After a couple of weeks, I called her and said, "Let's have dinner. I just want to visit with you."

The two weeks apart had proven to me that I couldn't live without her. I had decided, *I'm just going to ask her to marry me and see what happens.* Before dinner that night, I bought her a ring. I didn't just pick it up out of a case somewhere. I selected the diamond and took it to a jeweler to have it set in a beautiful mounting. This ring was really something!

I took Laurie to a nice restaurant. We chatted and dined by candlelight. All the while, I wondered how she might respond when I asked her to marry me. I had pushed her away only because I didn't want to hurt her, and I was concerned that I had pushed one time too many.

After dinner and dessert, I said, "I've got something here I'd like to give you." I opened the box and showed her the ring. "And I want to ask you something. Laurie, will you marry me?"

Laurie didn't play hard to get. She instantly said, "Yes!" We were both so excited!

We decided to keep our engagement a secret, so Laurie didn't wear her ring to work the next day. After nine years of our relationship, we wanted to surprise our friends. We were going to Bermuda for Ozark's year-end convention for our salespeople, and we planned to marry there. We told only a few close friends so they would be prepared to stand up with us at the wedding. Nobody else knew a thing about it.

> "I've got something here I'd like to give you." I opened the box and showed her the ring. "And I want to ask you something. Laurie, will you marry me?"

At the conference center in Bermuda, we carried out our plan. On the afternoon of December 30, 1989, we slid

wedding announcements under the doors of every Ozark employee there. It read: "Charlie and Laurie would like to invite you to attend their wedding."

People came that night in a state of shock! We had been dating so long they couldn't believe we were finally going to get married. Four hundred and fifty people came that night, and we bought dinner for the whole crowd. The man who married us was a political figure for Great Britain. He was calm and smooth at the ceremony, adding enough humor to spice up the event—as if it needed any spicing up!

Everybody was really excited. They were literally overjoyed for both of us. Laurie had become an integral part of the company as the head of the agency department, and people loved her. She had worked with almost every person there at the convention—the same ones who now attended our wedding—so they were very happy for her.

I wish I could say we went somewhere very romantic for our honeymoon. We talked about going off for a while, but Laurie said, "I really don't have time. I have too much work to do." I was busy, too, so we didn't go anywhere special until about a year later when we went to New York for three days.

Laurie sold her place, and she moved into my house. It all seemed so easy and natural at first because we had been together so often and so long over the past nine years. Surely there could be no surprises for us in our relationship!

But there were.

I honestly don't know what happened. I've thought about it a million times, but I can't figure it out. Not long after Laurie and I were married, we began drifting apart. I expected a lot more roses than thorns, but it seemed both of us were getting stuck far too often! Before long I thought, *If something doesn't happen soon, we're not going to make it!* She's a wonderful woman, and I think I am a decent person, but our marriage was deteriorating into a roommate relationship—and not a very good one at that.

We were very busy, but that wasn't the problem. Busyness may look like the real issue, but it is only a surface problem. I think it is used far too often as an excuse for laziness when people say, "I can't work so much because I've got to be with my family." That is absurd! No one has ever worked more than my dad, but I never felt closer to anybody in my life. When he was there with us, he was all there. Even if he wasn't physically there, I knew he was thinking of us and working hard for our welfare. People seldom drift apart because of work. They drift because they are not intimate, kind, and loving when they are around each other. Genuine love flourishes even in relatively short time spans when hearts connect and affection is expressed. Intimacy and warmth also grow when we have the courage to resolve conflict. That's the secret of it! Love takes much more than time; it takes heart. And love needs much more than physical proximity; it requires a willingness to listen, to give, and to forgive.

Affection erodes a bit every time we are miffed and we react by attacking or pulling into our shells. When we don't forgive, our natural instinct is to get even. We may try to get even by openly hurting the offender, or we may be much more subtle. We use sarcasm or gossip to get back at someone who has hurt us, and if someone confronts us, we try to deflect the blame by saying, "Oh, I was just kidding." But the damage is done.

But the greatest destroyer of relationships is indifference. We don't care enough to work through the problems and resolve the hurts, and every painful instance puts another brick in the wall between us and that other person. At first, the wall seems insignificant, but before long, it defines us and prevents any meaningful interaction. Scaling a low wall is much easier than waiting until it is ten feet tall!

Love is much more than a feeling. It is a commitment to meet another person's needs, whatever the cost to us. That's what Jesus did for us, and that's the standard of the love a man is to have for his wife. Paul wrote:

> Husbands, love your wives, just as Christ loved
> the church and gave Himself up for her to make
> her holy, cleansing her by the washing with water
> through the word, and to present her to Himself as
> a radiant church, without stain or wrinkle or any
> other blemish, but holy and blameless. In this same
> way, husbands ought to love their wives as their

own bodies. He who loves his wife loves himself.
After all, no one ever hated his own body, but he
feeds and cares for it, just as Christ does the church.
(Ephesians 5:25-29)

If we are radically committed to meeting the other's
needs first, love will grow. If we selfishly care primarily for
ourselves, relationships become clouded by anger, demands, and unrealistic expectations. Our spouses are our
greatest treasures! We need to guard, value, and protect
that treasure with an intense commitment.

In that same letter, Paul sought to remedy another
major problem in relationships: anger. He wrote:

In your anger do not sin. Do not let the sun go
down while you are still angry, and do not give the
devil a foothold. Get rid of all bitterness, rage and
anger, brawling and slander, along with every form
of malice. Be kind and compassionate to one another, forgiving each other, just as in Christ God
forgave you. (Ephesians 4:26-27, 31-32)

Paul acknowledges the reality of anger, but he gives
specific instructions about how to deal with it. Can anger
get a foothold in our lives? You bet it can! When we harbor
resentment toward someone who has hurt us, it festers in
our souls and robs us of the joy of our salvation and the joy
of every other relationship. Paul tells his readers (including you and me) to deal with it quickly, to root it out, and
to focus on God's great forgiveness of our own sins as the

motivation to forgive those who have sinned against us. These are powerful words . . . timely words.

But Laurie and I almost came to the point where we didn't even like each other! For about three years, we were just two people living in the same house. And I know there are millions of couples living just as we were! If that condition of their hearts doesn't change, they may eventually come to the conclusion that it's not worth it to continue.

Laurie and I experienced an ugly darkness in our lives. We thought about sleeping in separate rooms because we didn't want to be together. We never argued. Perhaps we should have argued more so we could get the problems out on the table and resolve them.

> For about three years, we were just two people living in the same house.

The traits in me that attracted her when we were dating were the things she began to despise the most—something that happens in many marriages. I was strong, always in charge, always up, never down, and never bitter. She loved those things about me for the nine years before we married, but when we got married, my strengths became threats. As Laurie pulled away from me, I just backed off. It wasn't what I wanted, but it's what I did, and I really didn't know how to fix the problem. We were in a vicious cycle. I would try to talk to her, but that irritated her because I talk too loud. She thought I was yelling at her—and maybe I was. I was trying my hardest to find an answer and somehow resolve the tension. Instead, I created even more tension between us.

I know I have a problem about how I come across to other people. At the office, I am often misunderstood. Once a young lady met me in the hall. Afterward, she told someone, "I don't know who that man was, but he was really upset." One of the other employees who knew me said, "Oh, that was just Charlie. He wasn't upset at all." If I come across to *strangers* that way, it's easy to see how Laurie would feel overwhelmed and intimidated by me. I'm trying to change in that area of my life!

Day after day, month after month, for three years, Laurie and I drifted apart until I made a fresh commitment to be giving instead of demanding. I resolved, "I am going to love this woman no matter what. If she responds well, that's great. If not, I'm not going to stop loving her. There's nothing in the world she can do to keep me from loving her!"

And I prayed, "Lord, You've got to help me love her! I can't do it in my own strength. Lord, I'm not going to try to change her. I'm going to love her just like she is." This commitment, this perspective, and this prayer have made all the difference in the world! Today our relationship is probably as strong as any couple's. Our relationship is a blessing from God!

> "There's nothing in the world she can do to keep me from loving her!"

If Laurie and I hadn't become Christians, I guarantee you we wouldn't be together. We were both ready to cash it in! We had tried everything, and we didn't know what else to do. But there was one more thing: God. At the bottom of the well, in our deepest pit, at the farthest extremity of our need, we cried out to God, and He worked a miracle in our lives.

CHAPTER 7

THE PRODIGAL RETURNS

When Laurie and I had been married almost two years, our marriage wasn't working. We had drifted apart, and nothing we tried seemed to fix it. Laurie was very unhappy. Every day her despair grew deeper and deeper. In November of 1992, Laurie desperately searched for anything that might help her make sense of her life. Her background is Catholic, so she started reading a Catholic prayer book to find some answers.

I knew the Lord was dealing with her. Even though I was far from God, the Holy Spirit spoke to me and said, "Look, Charlie. I'm trying to get Laurie's attention." At that point, I knew I could either be part of the solution or part of the problem. I knew the answer to Laurie's problem, but I wasn't sure if the answer to one problem might create new difficulties we couldn't resolve.

I asked Laurie to come into my office, and said, "Laurie, your Catholic prayer book may be helpful, but it can't meet your deepest need." She looked surprised, but I continued, "You need to invite Jesus into your heart."

I explained to Laurie that she needed to trust Christ to come into her life to forgive her sins. Then—and only then— she could find peace. She went alone to pray, but she came back and said, "Nothing happened." I told her to do it again. Still, she didn't feel anything had happened. Finally, one morning in her dressing room, she got on her knees and Jesus came into her heart. It was real! Laurie came into my office that morning and said, "It's done!"

I was thrilled, but I was also apprehensive. I knew what it takes for a new believer to become strong in the faith. When she left my office, I thought, *I've got to do something. If she does this by herself, she won't make it.*

A few days later, Laurie and I drove to New Life Community Church in Kansas City where my nephew, Jim Moore, is the pastor. I hadn't been to church in many years, except for funerals and weddings. I had taken a path far from God, far from His love and forgiveness I once experienced. Over time, my persistent, unrepented sins had separated me from God. I knew Laurie needed a Savior, but I also knew that I needed forgiveness, too. Now it was time to go for some personal business between myself and God. When Jim invited people to come forward after his message, Laurie and I both went. I made a public confession that I had come back to Christ.

> When she left my office, I thought, *I've got to do something. If she does this by herself, she won't make it.*

At the altar, I prayed, "Lord, I'm a sinner. I'm lost, and I need You to save me." When I prayed that prayer, it seemed like I had never been away from God at all. The glory of the Lord came on me. Immediately, I felt His joy and peace flood my heart, and I just couldn't hold it. I said out loud, "God, you are truly merciful!"

Now if I'd been God, I wouldn't have been so kind to a guy who had strayed for so many years, yet God gave me His peace and joy in that instant. I'll never forget it. At that moment, I understood the Parable of the Prodigal Son better than anybody in the world.

Laurie was surprised at my response. I could tell she was a little worried about me, so I told her, "I promise I'm not going to go crazy. I'm just going to go to church and worship and grow in my faith in Jesus. Don't worry. I won't talk to everybody I see about it."

That didn't last very long. I went back into the office on Monday and told everybody in the building what had happened—not only what happened to me but to Laurie, too. I needed to tell them because I was bursting with the love of God in my heart. One of the greatest instruments Satan uses is the threat of rejection. We are excited about the grace of God, but Satan whispers to us, "OK, you've done it. Now just shut up about it or people will think you're a fanatic. . . . And nobody likes fanatics!" But I didn't listen to his whispers. I told everybody who had ears!

> I was bursting with the love of God in my heart.

A lot of people I told were very excited about my new faith, but some were a little uncomfortable with it. They said, "Charlie, I think that's really nice . . . for you." Those who were Christians were just as excited as I was (maybe they'd been praying for me), but others were confused and concerned.

Over a period of time, they begin to notice changes in me. I had never been one to use the Lord's name in vain or rant and rave, so there weren't those kinds of changes, but I began to talk about my relationship with the Lord so people would know what great things God had done in my life. It didn't take long before I started really praying for the employees—and people started getting saved. When we went to our conventions, I preached a sermon every time, and we always had people saved! We have people saved every year at our annual sales convention.

My return to Christ has given me a fresh perspective on the goodness of God. More than ever, I am convinced that God is sovereign. He orchestrates some events to accomplish His purposes, and sometimes He allows our mistakes—even our greatest sins—to be woven into the fabric of His mercy in our lives. I have a sneaking suspicion that after his return and reconciliation, the prodigal in Luke 15 was more intent on pleasing his father than he ever was before. He was so appreciative of his father's goodness, forgiveness, and generosity, he wanted to please him in every way possible. In fact, I can imagine that he was extravagant in honoring his father, and he daydreamed about how he might honor him more. That is the

motivation I have for honoring God whose goodness, forgiveness, and generosity have been so lavishly poured out
on me.

Many people, even many sincere Christians, are confused about how they can know God's will for their lives.
We can't know God's will if we don't know Him and love
Him. For example, I know Laurie's will most of the time
because I know her so well. If we are in a restaurant and
the waiter comes by to ask for drink orders while Laurie
has gone to the restroom, I can tell him what she wants
because I've been with her many times and I know what
she likes. In other cases, like which wallpaper she wants to
put up, I take the time to ask her and listen to her. Again,
the relationship lets me know what her will is. I'm very
interested in her will because I know if I please her, things
go much better between us. I care for her very much, and I
want to please her.

It's exactly the same way with God. If I love Him and
spend time with Him, then I'll be sensitive to Him. I can't
be sensitive to Him if I don't love Him and become familiar with His wants and His ways. Everything comes back
to loving Him. At one point, Jesus was confronted by some
lawyers. They knew He was teaching about truth that went
beyond the rigid laws of the Old Testament. He was talking about a new kind of relationship with God. Matthew
wrote:

> Hearing that Jesus had silenced the Sadduccees,
> the Pharisees got together. One of them, an expert

in the law, tested Him with this question: "Teacher, which is the greatest commandment in theLaw?"

Jesus replied, " 'Love the Lord your God with all your heart and with all your soul and with all your mind.' This is the first and greatest commandment. And the second is like it: 'Love your neighbor as yourself.' All the Law and the Prophets hang on these two commandments." (Matthew 22:34-40)

Do you want to know what the will of God is? The most important aspect of His will isn't confusing at all: it is to love Him with all your heart, soul, and mind. That's right! Loving Him is His will. Then, in the rich context of that relationship, He can say to you, "My child, I want you to do this or that." The deeper we know Him, the more sensitive we will be to His speaking to our hearts. I want to get to the place where He only needs to whisper for me to know what He wants. At first He may need to yell a little, and maybe tap us on the shoulder a few times to get our attention. As the relationship matures and we know His Word more deeply, however, we are more in tune with His heart and His desires.

> Do you want to know what the will of God is? The most important aspect of His will isn't confusing at all: it is to love Him with all your heart, soul, and mind. That's right! Loving Him is His will.

As we obey His voice and we see Him work in and through us, we become even more sensitive to Him. On the other hand, when we disobey, it is like trying to listen to a friend speak quietly in the car when the radio is blasting rock music. Disobedience is noise in our relationship with God. It clouds our minds and muffles our ability to hear. If it persists long enough, we get to the point where we can hardly hear God's voice at all.

Some people make a common error in discerning God's will. They believe they should sit passively until God shows them what to do. I've noticed people's inactivity and asked them, "What are you doing?"

They have replied, "I am just waiting on God to know His will."

"How long you been waiting?"

"Oh, about a year."

"What have you been doing in the meantime?"

"Nothing. Just waiting."

"Friend," I tell them, "this isn't the way! God never uses anybody who isn't busy! You can't turn a car if it isn't moving, and God can't steer a Christian if he isn't active."

Certainly, we need to be quiet and still so we can hear His "still, small voice," but that doesn't mean we have to be entirely immobile. We need to be busy doing the things we know He wants us to do, like providing for our families, helping the needy, reading the Bible, praying, and serving God. When we are already walking, it is much easier for God to show us the next step.

When people talk about "God's will," most are referring to activities and direction. But God's will is first and foremost a deep, loving, encouraging relationship with Him, out of which comes direction in life.

God wants us to be busy making a living, and if we have enough money that we don't have to make a living, we need to be busy helping people. Doing nothing while seeking God's will is a paradox. It simply doesn't make sense.

The Scriptures speak of "waiting on the Lord," but let's not misunderstand the lesson. One of the most beloved of these passages is in Isaiah 40:

> Yet those who wait for the Lord will gain new strength;
> They will mount up with wings like eagles,
> They will run and not get tired,
> They will walk and not become weary.
> (Isaiah 40:31 New American Standard Bible)

The concept of "waiting on the Lord" doesn't have much to do with time; it refers more to our attitude of expectancy. We don't just kill time as we wait for God to show us what He wants us to do. Instead, we focus on His faithfulness, His grace, and His power, and our faith is encouraged to believe that He will accomplish whatever we need Him to do in, for, and through us. We pray in our closets earnestly, but we also remain in His presence all day, anticipating Him to be loving and strong on our behalf because that is His nature.

I spend time in prayer every morning, listening, talking, interacting with my Heavenly Father. Sometimes I don't really have much to say. I tell the Lord, "I don't have a lot today, but I just want to be in Your presence. I'm just going to show up and be with You." Soon, the Spirit of the Lord starts moving on me, and He puts praise and petitions on my heart. To me, this is "waiting on the Lord."

Some of us think that the supernatural life means God must do miraculous things to provide for our needs. Sometimes He does some unusual things. He commanded ravens to bring food for Elijah, but I've never had birds show up at the farm to give me something to eat. But God has given me wisdom and strength to make enough money to provide for the family. In both cases, God provided. Is one less significant than the other? I don't think so. Sometimes God chooses to act in a way that is outside the normal expectations of life, but most often He involves us in the process and requires us to depend on Him, thinking and working hard to accomplish His will.

Communication with God is vital if the relationship is to be strong and intimate. Jesus instructed us to go in our closets and close the door to pray. I believe that! We need undistracted solitude to learn to listen to God, and to listen to our own hearts so we can praise, petition, or repent. Prayer is wonderfully uplifting, but it can also be hard work! I do not believe you can adequately intercede for others while you drive a car, wash dishes, or do anything else in your daily routine. When I'm driving a car, that is my main job—and everybody on the road with me hopes I'm paying attention to that job. While I'm driving, I can pray—and I do—but I have to make sure my mind is focused primarily on driving safely. I've heard people say, "I pray all the time." But for many of them, the truth is that they pray very little. I read or hear on the radio or television that people are redefining prayer: "Walking is a form of prayer," or "Breathing is a form of prayer," or "Everything I do is a kind of prayer." I have no clue what these people are talking about . . . and I'm sure they don't either. Certainly we can pray when we walk, and we'd sure better be breathing when we pray! But prayer is far more than walking and breathing. It is coming to the throne of the King of the Universe . . . who is also our loving Father and our dearest Friend.

When we go before God, He is so all consuming that we forget everything else. Many people don't have a lofty view of God at all. They see Him as only a little bigger than they are. Our Lord is truly awesome. In fact, I believe we should never use that term any other way except when we are speaking of God. He inspires awe. We are overcome with His greatness and gentleness, His majesty and His tenderness. The word *awesome* is used much too frivolously by most people these days. It really applies only to God. As the Rich Mullins song says, "Our God is an awesome God!" We will comprehend that fact if we spend enough time alone with Him. Then His glory permeates every moment and aspect of our lives. The Spirit and the power of God consume us—and we become incredibly motivated and content.

Sometimes I think it might be better if we lived under the rule of a king so we would better understand God as our King. In our democracy (and believe me, I love our country) we have exalted man instead of God. If we lived in a kingdom, perhaps we would have the sense that it is an awesome thing to be in the presence of God! And of course, God is a far greater king than any the world has ever seen. Caesar, Charlemagne, Ghengis Khan, and Arthur are like bugs next to God. And He is not only our king, He is our creator, sustainer, provider, and ultimately, our Savior. We look to Him to save our souls. What king can do that? And His intentions are not whimsical or evil; they're always good. Look at the kings throughout history. Most of them were tyrants, and yet our heavenly King has the best of intentions for us and is even willing to be called our "Friend."

This perspective radically affects our prayers. We can approach Him as a Friend, but at the same time, we approach Him as the Creator, as the lover of our souls, as our provider who is able to meet every need. He can give us joy even while we are in trials and troubles. Nobody else can do that—only God!

My brother Wilbur recently died of cancer. Even in his last months as he daily faced excruciating pain and certain death, he told me over and over again, "Charlie, God has been so good to me!" He had perfect joy even while he was dying, a joy that came from God. Wilbur understood what

> But prayer is far more than walking and breathing. It is coming to the throne of the King of the Universe . . . who is also our loving Father and our dearest Friend.

I'm trying to say. He experienced God's grace and mercy even (and especially) in the midst of his pain. That grace and mercy are just as available to you and me today.

Another wonderful evidence of the grace of God is the story of Paul Casey. I hired Paul in 1964 just after we began Ozark. He had been with another insurance company, and when he joined us, he jumped in with both feet. From the beginning he worked very hard and accomplished a lot. We promoted him to district manager, and soon we made him a zone manager. By the early 70s, Paul became one of the Vice Presidents along with Hugh Wyatt. During that time, I had my financial problems with the real estate venture in San Antonio. My credibility was shaken in the eyes of some of our people—and one of those people was Paul. He knew I had done nothing illegal or unethical, but he also knew I had exercised poor judgment in that investment. Paul wanted—in fact, he demanded—more freedom to make decisions for the company.

By 1975 we had allowed our operations to be decentralized, but I realized that strategy wasn't working very well. Our sales were slipping, so I brought some aspects of field authority back into our national office. The rest of our top management, such as Hugh Wyatt, agreed with that policy, but Paul and Jewell Barlow were terribly upset with that decision. They accused me of being unfair to them, and in their anger, they both resigned from the company. Both men were terribly bitter, and they sued me for five million dollars.

This was a tough time for me. I had lost everything through bankruptcy, and Bob Shaw was not fulfilling his promises to me. Now, in addition, two of those I had hired and promoted were suing me. The case went to court, but the judge threw it out because their case was worthless. Paul and Jewell had to pay their legal fees, so their suit cost them a good bit of money. Jewell and Paul went into business together after that, but soon their relationship soured and they parted.

About ten years later, I was standing in a crowd at a political rally, and Paul Casey walked up to me. I hadn't seen him in years, and it startled me to see him walking toward me. I didn't know what he was going to do, but he said, "Charlie, there's something I want to say to you, and I want these people to hear me." I nodded for him to go ahead. He looked me in the eye and said, "I want you to forgive me for what I've done to you. I was wrong."

I told him, "Paul, I've already forgiven you, but I'm glad to let you and these other people here know that I've forgiven you."

It took a lot of courage for Paul to come to me like he did and admit he was wrong. I'll always remember that day.

After we started Heartland Community Church, Paul and his

Paul Casey sings to his 92 year-old sister

Paul was still smiling even in his last months

wife Martha came from Kansas City to attend services. They had not called to say they were coming, so I was surprised when I saw them walk through the door. As I preached my sermon that morning, and Paul leaned over to Martha and said, "You know, I don't think I have a relationship with Jesus." A minute later, Paul and Martha both came to the altar and knelt to receive Christ as their Savior and Lord. I prayed the sinner's prayer with Paul, and in front of my eyes, this man was gloriously saved! That was one of the most touching sights I've ever seen in my life.

Paul and Martha moved from Kansas City to Florida, but since that day at Heartland, he stayed in touch with me. In December of 1998, Paul visited Heartland and came to the altar to ask for prayer for healing. He knew he was sick with a severe strain of leukemia. That night he collapsed and was taken to the hospital. I've visited many people in hospitals over the years, but I've never seen a man who had such peace and joy on his face. I went in to bless him, but instead, he blessed me. This man was ready to go to heaven. Over and over again, he told me, "Charlie, Jesus is so good to me!"

Paul Casey died the next day. I preached at his funeral. It was one of the most meaningful days of my life. What a story of repentance and love! Paul Casey had the humility to admit he was wrong, and God worked His great grace in that man's heart.

TAYSIR S. ABU SAADA

—Former Palestinian
Freedom Fighter

I met Charlie Sharpe in 1974 in Kansas City. I was working as a dishwasher at La Mediterraneé, an exclusive French restaurant. One day I was promoted to busboy, but I was terribly nervous to go to a table of customers to take away their dishes. What if I spilled something on them? I would be so embarrassed! On that day, the first table I went to was Charlie's. My knees were shaking! As I reached for his dish, I said, "Excuse me, sir."

He looked at me with that beautiful smile of his and said, "Thank you, young man."

His kindness was like a drink of cool water to me. I felt so much more comfortable after he spoke to me. He was so kind to take time away from his dinner and his companions to thank me for taking his dishes. I am from the Middle East, and I never thanked the servants in my father's house. I took them for granted and expected a lot from them without any word of encouragement or thanks, but Charlie Sharpe didn't take me for granted. That meant so much to me.

From that day on, I looked for Charlie every time he came to the restaurant. Even when he didn't sit in my station, I talked to the other busboys to be sure they looked out for him. And they did. Later, I became a waiter, and I often served Charlie and his parties. I found out that he was asking his secretary to request me when she called to make reservations, and of course, that meant a great deal to me. Eventually I became a maitre d' at La Mediterraneé, and I seated Charlie in special areas of the restaurant. Every time he came, our relationship developed. I began to seek his advice on personal matters from time to time, and he helped me a lot. I called him at his office, and we had lunches together so I could talk to him.

I remember when Charlie bought his office building for the insurance company. It looked so old and shabby. I asked him if he was going to tear it down and build a new one, but he said, "Oh, no. I'm going to fix it up. It'll be beautiful!" He took me to a corner of the interior where the inch-thick dust had been cleaned off. The building was a piece of art under all that dust! He had a vision to make something unusable into something beautiful. He's still doing that today with people's lives.

I grew to like and respect Charlie Sharpe, and then I grew to really love him. He always spoke to and treated me with kindness, and he spoke the same way to those around him at his table and to the waiters at the restaurant. He was the same way with his salespeople. No matter how difficult the situation (and I know in business, things get very tense sometimes), he always remained calm and spoke to people with respect and kindness. I have seen many successful businessmen. They have to be heartless and tough in order to make it, but that's not how Charlie is at all. Because I have seen his kindness and integrity over many years, I learned to trust Charlie completely.

When I tell how I became a Christian, I use my relationship with Charlie as an illustration. I tell how God uses people to show us His love, kindness, and trustworthiness. God knew my heart. He knew I needed to see love in action. He used Charlie to show Himself to me. When it was time for me to understand about Jesus, God used a man I had learned to trust to show me the way. At the time, I wasn't seeking God. I had been trained by the Palestinian Liberation Organization to kill Jews.

In September of 1992, my daughter asked me to teach her about Islam. I took a copy of the Muslim holy book, the Koran, from the mantle in our home, and I told her where to begin reading to prepare for our discussions. From that moment, I felt a sudden and deep emptiness in my heart. For some reason, I called a Jewish rabbi to help answer my questions. (I have no idea why I called a rabbi. After all, I was trained to kill people of his race.) This rabbi was one of my customers at the restaurant, and I knew him well. I hoped he would point me in the right way. I called him and said, "Rabbi, I feel such emptiness. I don't know what's going on. Can you help me?"

He responded, "Well, Tass, we are getting close to Christmas, and many people feel anxiety during this season. Perhaps that's the problem."

"I don't know why I would feel anxious," I told him. "I have everything I want. I have money. I have a nice home. My family is doing well. I like my job."

He said, "I don't know, then. Why don't we get together for lunch so we can talk about it?"

"Okay, let's meet soon," I told him.

But I never called him. A few months later, our restaurant developed problems with our landlord in the exclusive Country Club Plaza. We decided to look for a new location. Charlie knew I planned to own the restaurant in a few years, so he was advising me about our new location. He came into the restaurant during the last week in February, and he said, "Tass, there is a place on Broadway called The Villa. I think you should go look at it. That would be a very good location for you."

I told him, "Charlie, three days ago, the chef, our contractor, and I went to that place, but as soon as I walked in the door, I felt the creeps. I couldn't wait to get out of there! That place used to be a funeral home."

Charlie laughed for a second or two, then he became serious. He looked me straight in the eyes and boldly said, "Do you know why you feel that way, Tass? It's because you don't have the fear of God in your heart."

That comment struck me. Telling a Muslim that he doesn't have the fear of God in his heart took a lot of courage, but I loved him so much that I didn't get defensive at all. I said, "Charlie, I'm a Muslim. Surely I fear God."

"No, Tass. If you feared God, you wouldn't be afraid in that building. Don't worry. I can help you with that." With his finger pointing to the sky, he told me, "I've got connections."

I laughed and said, "Yeah, sure."

That was the first time Charlie had ever talked about spiritual things with me. I had no idea he was a spiritual person. I had seen him drink wine, and I had seen him at the restaurant with many different women. As a Muslim, I couldn't understand why he was now talking to me about God. I found out later that Charlie and Laurie had become Christians only weeks before.

It dawned on me that Charlie and Laurie had changed in some ways. They used to drink a bottle or a bottle and a half of wine with their meals, but now they didn't. And now Charlie was talking to me about God. At the time, I didn't understand the relationship between their new behavior and his comments about God, but later, I understood.

For the next three weeks I wondered, *What is that "connection" Charlie was talking about?* I saw him with Laurie the next week at the restaurant, and I asked him about it. For a long time, I had assumed that Charlie was a Jew because his last name sounded Jewish to me. I walked over to his table and asked him, "Charlie, you said you have 'connections.' What were you talking about?"

He said, "Tass, this isn't a good time for us to talk. The restaurant is crowded, and you are very busy. Let's get together next week to discuss it."

But I didn't call him.

That next week, I saw him again at the restaurant. By this time, my heart was even more troubled. I was confused, and I was losing focus. My mind was obsessed with finding out what Charlie's connection was. I walked up to his table, and I said, "Charlie, I really need to know what your connection is. Please explain it to me."

Charlie said, "Tass, I'll be happy to tell you, but we can't talk about it in a busy place like this. We need to talk in private. Please call me so we can meet next week."

I said, "Okay, I'll call you."

I was still very troubled, but for some reason, I still didn't call him. That was one of the most difficult weeks of my life. My mind wandered away from my work and my family. The only thing I could think about was the emptiness in my heart and the hope of finding Charlie's connection to fill it. At times, my wife Karen had to lead me around like a little child because I was so preoccupied with my troubled heart that I couldn't function normally.

That next week was our last one for the La Mediterraneé at our site in the Country Club Plaza. People from all over the country flew in to have dinner there one last time. I guess they had so many happy memories there, they wanted to cherish the moment one last time. On Saturday night, the place was packed. Charlie and Laurie came in, and I seated them. I could clearly see their table. Laurie got up and walked past me on her way to the restroom. I thought, *This is my opportunity. Charlie is alone. I must go talk to him!*

I walked to his table, and I got on my knees next to Charlie at his table. I was so disturbed. I was like an empty shell, and I was desperate. Getting on my knees next to Charlie was a sign of my sense of need.

I put my hand in his hand, and I pleaded, "Charlie, I've got to know this connection. I'm so messed up I can't eat, I can't sleep, and I can't think. I have to know."

Charlie looked a bit uncomfortable. I guess he was nervous with me kneeling next to him and pleading with him in a crowded restaurant. He tried to pull his hand away, but I insisted, "You're not going to get away from me!"

He told me gently, "Tass, get up. Calm down.... This is not the time and place. We must talk somewhere else. Please call me Monday and we'll meet."

"No, I can't wait until Monday."

"Then call me tomorrow at home at 1:30."

I nodded, "I'll call you." I grasped his hand tightly to show my thanks for his willingness to meet me, then I got up and walked back to my place.

The next day, I anticipated the hour I would call him, but my mind was so obsessed, I actually missed the time. I looked at my watch, and it was 1:35. I thought, *Oh no, I've missed him! He may have left!* I ran and quickly dialed the phone, and to my relief, Charlie answered.

He asked, "How are you doing, Tass?"

"Terrible," I answered. "I can't even drive. Will you come pick me up?"

"Sure. I'll be there in twenty minutes."

Charlie arrived and picked me up, then we drove to his house in Kansas City. We walked in, and Charlie said, "Tass, to have the peace I have, you must love a Jew."

I was dumbfounded. Charlie knew all about me. He knew I hated Jews. I was trained to kill them, so when Charlie said I would have to love one, I was heartbroken. I moaned audibly, then I muttered, "There is no way on earth I can love a Jew. Why are you saying this to me?"

Charlie motioned for me to sit near him on a sofa, then he asked, "Tell me, what do you know about Jesus Christ?"

I replied, "I know of Jesus. Muslims believe he was a prophet. We respect him as one of the great men before Mohammed."

"But He's more than that. He's God."

I reacted, "Now hold it right there. I don't believe that. Now you are really not making sense." I paused, then I asked, "Is this all you wanted to tell me?"

"Cool down, Tass. Hold on. Let me explain some things to you." Charlie got his Bible and put it down between us. As soon as he put it down, I jumped away from it.

He was startled, "Why did you do that?"

"I can't touch that!"

"Why not? It's just pieces of paper."

"No, it's not. It has God's name on it."

Charlie was surprised by my response. "So you believe this is God's Word?"

"Yes. Yes, I do."

I have no idea why I answered that way. As a Muslim, I certainly didn't believe the Christian Bible was God's Word. Muslims believe the Bible is no longer valid because it has been changed by man, but I had said I believed it. As soon as those words came out of my mouth, I wondered why I had said them.

Charlie told me, "Since you believe this is the Word of God, let me show you what the Word of God says about Jesus Christ. Fair enough?"

"Fair enough."

Charlie opened to the Gospel of John and began to read in chapter one. Something hit me, and I began to shake. After a few moments, I blacked out. I have no idea how long I was out or how long Charlie read. All I remember hearing was the first verse:

> In the beginning was the Word, and the Word was with God, and the Word was God. He was with God in the beginning.

Then I blacked out. The next thing I knew, I was on my knees on the floor with my hands lifted up. I heard myself praying to Jesus Christ asking Him to be my Lord and Savior. At that moment, I felt as if a mountain had been lifted off my shoulders. I felt such relief! I looked at Charlie sitting on the sofa. Streams of tears flowed from his face. I asked him, "Charlie, why are you crying?"

He smiled broadly, "Man, I've never seen anything like this!"

He hugged me, and we both cried tears of joy. After a few moments, he asked me, "Tass, do you know what you just did? Without me telling you, you called Jesus 'Lord and Savior.' You have accepted Christ and become a Christian."

"I did?"

"Yes," he smiled. "I know. I was there when it happened!"

"What happened to me?" I asked.

"You got off the sofa, and you got on your knees. You opened your eyes and lifted up your hands, and you prayed in English to invite Christ into your life."

I told him, "Charlie, I feel like a mountain was lifted off my shoulders."

"Praise the Lord! That's Christ," Charlie explained. "He came into your life, forgave you, and gave you peace. These are signs of your salvation."

After I got home from Charlie's house, I told Karen I had trusted Christ. She was skeptical. She said, "Yeah, sure." She had watched me do a lot of crazy things in our nineteen years of marriage, and our relationship wasn't all that great. I had tried to break away from her before, but my heart didn't let me.

The day after I received Christ, my eighteen-year-old son was in the bathroom shaving. I went in and said to him, "Son, I want to tell you about something that happened to me."

He had shaving cream all over his face, and he looked at me, "What's that, Dad?"

"Yesterday, I accepted Jesus Christ as my Lord and Savior. Son, I'm a Christian."

His big beautiful eyes grew even larger. He exclaimed, "Oh, Dad! I'm so happy for you!" He grabbed me and hugged me. We stood there in the bathroom hugging and crying for a long time, then I realized something was strange. My son was a Muslim, too. He shouldn't be happy I had become a Christian!

I asked him, "Son, why are you so happy for me?"

"Dad," he grinned, "three months ago, I accepted Christ. I'm a Christian, too!"

That was a beautiful moment for both of us. God had given him the wisdom to keep his commitment to Christ from me. He knew I would have killed him, or at the least, I would have disowned him and kicked him out of our house. But now, both of us were believers. What a joy!

After 45 days, Karen was convinced that my transformation was real. I was consumed by the Word of God. I woke up reading the Bible, and I went to sleep reading the Bible. In between, I read the Bible. The changes she saw in me led her to think about her own salvation, and she responded to Christ.

Charlie knew I needed to learn and grow a lot, so he took me to his church in Kansas City so I could hear the Word of God taught clearly and boldly. I got good teaching and a solid foundation from pastor Jim Moore. And I learned a lot from Charlie. I didn't know for all those years that Charlie had been a pastor long before. Now he was teaching about Christ again, and I was learning a lot from him.

Over the months and years, God worked in my heart and called me to be a missionary to my people in Saudi Arabia and the Middle East. We responded to that call, and we began to prepare mentally, physically, and spiritually for that calling. I moved from La Mediterraneé to run a small cafe, and we began to make plans to leave the United States.

Four years after I trusted Christ, Charlie invited Karen and me to come to Heartland to go to church with them. Charlie had invited me many times over the years to come to visit him at the farm, but I had never come. On this Sunday, Karen and I came and worshiped, then we went home. Early the next Sunday morning, I told her, "Why don't we go to Heartland Church today?" Again, we drove from Kansas City to Northeast Missouri to go to church. For some reason we were drawn to Heartland, but I didn't know why.

One day, Charlie came to my cafe in Kansas City, and he asked me, "Why don't you and your family move to the farm and join us?"

I said, "Charlie, you know God has called us to go overseas." We were downsizing, getting ready to go to the Middle East to tell Muslims about Jesus.

"Do whatever the Lord is calling you to do," Charlie assured me. "Just pray about it and do what He tells you."

I responded, "I know what he's calling me to do."

"Fine. Do it with all your heart."

But Karen and I kept going to Heartland often because we were drawn there. One Saturday morning, I got up at four o'clock and drove to Heartland. On the way, I prayed intensely and drove slowly. I arrived at Heartland at about nine o'clock. I walked to a spot near the lake below the school. At the time, only a few foundations of the houses and the school were there—nothing else. I prayed, "Lord, I am so confused I don't know what to do. I feel drawn to Heartland, but there are no Muslims here. God, You know this can't be for me. I know You have called me to reach Muslims. I need a sign from You to show me what You want."

I stayed at that spot from nine o'clock in the morning until about three o'clock in the afternoon. At that point, God opened His heart to me and showed me, "This is the place I want you to be. This is where I will build the foundation for missions." It was almost like God projected His vision for what

He is going to do at Heartland on a screen so I wouldn't miss it. It was that clear.

I got up, and I said, "Thank You, Lord." I got in my car and drove straight back to Kansas City to tell my wife. I didn't even stop to tell Charlie what God had shown me. He was only ten minutes from the lake, but I didn't stop to tell him about the vision. I arrived at home and I said, "Karen, I really believe God wants us at Heartland. I don't know why. There are no Muslims there, and I don't understand how we will reach Muslims from there, but I believe He wants us to go there. Start praying and see what God says to you."

On Monday, Charlie came to my cafe. I told him about my trip to Heartland on Saturday and the vision God gave me. He smiled, "You came all the way to Heartland, and you didn't come by to see me?"

"I wanted to see Karen first and ask her to pray," I explained. "She's still not settled in her heart about the decision to go to Heartland. The Lord will speak to her."

And the Lord spoke to Karen to confirm His leading us to Heartland, so we moved to Heartland in January of 1997. Charlie asked me to be in charge of the kitchen at the school. I would like to say that I sensed God's peace about our decision, but I didn't. My heart was in turmoil for the first six months. I was so confused. Even though God had shown me a clear vision, my heart deceived me. I kept thinking, *What are you doing here? How can you reach Muslims from this place?*

I prayed, "Lord, if I have made a mistake by coming here, please show me. God, please harden Charlie and Laurie's hearts against me so they will throw me out of Heartland if You want me to leave." I looked for this to happen, but after I prayed, Charlie and Laurie showed me even more love than ever!

One day I was watching the young people come through the lunch line, and I realized how God was working so powerfully in their hearts. As I looked at their faces, I could see many who had been withdrawn or angry when they first came to Heartland and were now experiencing the love of Jesus. I saw each of them every day, and God was allowing me to build relationships with them. Many were opening themselves to me and allowing me to minister to them. I was giving love, and I was receiving their love. It was incredible!

I went to tell Charlie about this encouragement. I told him, "I have struggled ever since Karen and I came here."

Charlie nodded, "I know you have, Tass."

I told him about watching the young people as they came through the lunch line, and I explained how that had warmed my heart. Charlie responded, "Praise the Lord! You just had a breakthrough! God gave you a victory."

Last March, I flew to Cyprus to speak to a group of missionaries who share Christ with Muslims in Arab countries. Some of the missionaries were Arab Christians, some were Americans, and some were Europeans. During the conference, I had heard many of them talk about their needs in their ministries. As I was speaking to them, God gave me a vision. All of the skills we teach young men and women here at Heartland are desperately needed in those Arab countries! Saudi Arabia and the United Arab Emirates have the two largest dairies in the world. They are in need of skilled workers. Many of those countries are constructing many buildings and roads, and they need workers to help them. They need drivers for heavy equipment, managers of food and beverage operations, and many other skills we teach. In the middle of my talk to these missionaries, I stopped and told them, "Guys, we have the capacity at Heartland to train Muslim converts in many skills that are in demand in the Middle East and then send them back as missionaries to the countries where they are called to minister. That is God's vision."

I came back and shared this vision with Charlie, and he responded typically, "Great! Go do whatever it takes to fulfill that vision!"

Today, we are beginning to lay the foundation to train Muslim converts in these skills to equip them to go to the Middle East. Some of these converts come from that part of the world, but many will come from

America. This country is a target for Muslim missionaries, and many Muslims have moved here. In 1974, a Muslim leaders' conference was held in Mecca. These men formed a plan to send thousands of Muslims to America to win this country for Islam. In those years, they have made incredible progress. A Muslim opened Congress with a prayer to Allah, and last year, Hillary Clinton held a reception to celebrate the Muslim holy feast in the White House. Islam is the fastest growing religion in the world, and it is making tremendous strides in this country.

Charlie is 100 percent supportive of God's call on my life. He is the one who led me to Christ, the one I have trusted all these years, and the one who encourages my faith now. Today my wife, my son, and my daughter are all believers and they are serving the Lord. My daughter is studying to be a teacher, and she wants to be a missionary. My son is going through The Shepherd's School, and he is helping to establish a new church. For a father, there is no more joy than to see my children walk in the truth.

A few years ago, I talked to my father in Qatar. I told him, "Dad, you are so much against me for converting to Christianity. Let me share something with you. When I was a Muslim, I sinned against God, but none of you told me I needed to stop sinning against God. Now that I have found the true God, my life has changed. I pray, I fast, I give, I love,

I praise God and worship Him, but now you tell me I am sinning against God. That just doesn't make sense."

I love my father and my mother, and I am praying that God's mercy will fall on them so they will come to know Jesus. I am willing to give my life for their souls.

For all those years I was with the restaurant in Kansas City, I met many, many wealthy people— most of them were Jews. They were so kind to me. They trusted me, and they wanted me to take care of them. During all this time, I held bitter resentment against them. Because of my position at the restaurant, I only smiled at them and served them. I wanted to poison their food, but I didn't want to lose my job. Now I know that God was protecting me. Some of them sent me to their personal tailors and had custom suits made for me . . . incredibly beautiful suits. But I still hated them.

When I invited Christ into my heart, God put in my heart a burden to pray—not for the Muslims, but for the Jews first. God gave me a genuine love for them. After that time, in all my interactions with Jews, I showed love to them. It was amazing grace! I realized, *I don't hate these people anymore. God is at work in my life! I don't understand what happened, but hatred had been cleansed by a Jew, Jesus Christ.* Nothing on earth can cleanse the heart of a Palestinian toward a Jew. Only Christ's grace can do that. When I saw that, I was again assured of the work of salvation in my life.

After I got saved, I went to the Jews who came to our restaurant to tell them I had trusted Jesus to be my Savior. They told me, "Hey, that's our Messiah!"

All of a sudden, they wanted to claim Jesus as their own! God said He would make the Jewish people jealous, and He is using people like me to do a work in their hearts to show them Jesus is real.

I told them, "For years I hated you because you were Jews."

"But we didn't know that," they replied.

"I couldn't show my hatred because I needed a job. But now I love you. I truly love you!" It blew them away.

I went to the Jewish temples and synagogues to study the Torah. They asked me why I came to them since I was a Palestinian, so I told them my testimony. I trust God used me in their lives.

Years ago, I lived in the Middle East. I was dedicated to destroying God's chosen people in the land God has given them. Today, I live in the middle of a corn field, and I am dedicated to reaching those people who taught me to hate with the incredible love of Jesus Christ.

Before Heartland, farm work and friendship, 1972

CHAPTER 8

HEARTLAND

I had been buying land in northeast Missouri, near the town of LaBelle, since the 1960s. Around 1988, before Laurie and I were married, I bought the land where our school is today. Not long afterward, I was driving down the road across the lake by myself in a Ford pickup, and the thought came to me out of nowhere: *What a place to do something for young people!* I envisioned a camp setting. I had never worked with young people before, but the image was clear and strong. I have always tried to do things to help people, so I just thought it was another Charlie Sharpe idea. I didn't realize this time it was a calling from God.

The thought was real, but it didn't last. Over the next days, weeks, and months, I forgot all about it. Then in the spring of 1993, soon after I had recommitted my life to Christ, I was driving on the same road again. When I came to the same exact spot, the Spirit of the Lord spoke to me and said: "Now, Charlie, you can hear Me. It's Me talking.

Build this place for the young people." In my spirit, I saw a building for kids as plain as day.

In 1994, I drove by that same spot, and God gave me a vision of hundreds of young people. They were a long way away, and I couldn't see any faces, but I was sure they were young people. They were on their knees with their hands up praising God. I thought I was losing it!

The image was vivid and real, but it was over in an instant. I don't know if this was a vision like the prophets had, but it sure got my attention! I had told Laurie about my second experience of seeing the camp, but she wasn't too excited about it. She told people, "I run the insurance company. Charlie is taking care of things out at the farm."

> I don't know if this was a vision like the prophets had, but it sure got my attention!

She was interested in doing her work at Ozark in the agency department, and she simply wasn't interested in leaving that important work to do anything else . . . until I told her about the third encounter. When I told her about the hundreds of young people with their arms raised in praise to God, her heart suddenly changed. Now she wanted to be a part of it.

Our vision for Heartland began to form. Slowly but steadily, the components seemed to take shape: the church, the school, the farm, the Recovery Center. . . and they all seemed to fit together so well. God seemed to have His hand on us to guide us in our planning. We would establish a community of faith centered around the school and the church. Many of those in our Heartland community would come from the surrounding towns and farms, but many more would move to Heartland to work and live there. Troubled young people could come to be a part of the Recovery Center, and they would learn responsibility by working as farm hands after school. The Lord gave us that vision, and we believed He would bring all the pieces together in a way that honored Him.

We wanted to start Heartland Community Church in 1995, so we began to look for a pastor who would lead our people. We wanted someone who had a heart for the truth of the Scriptures, as well as compassion for the lost and hurting. We talked about different people, but as our search continued, God put it on my heart to be the pastor. At first, I rigidly resisted this call. After all, I had been a pastor once before and let my people down. I didn't want to let anybody else down. I had a million reasons and excuses for God to find somebody else, but as I prayed, I sensed God was calling me—not someone else, but me—to pastor this church. I had talked to a lot of people over the past few years about obeying the Lord, so I had no choice but to practice what I'd been preaching to them.

We began the church, and I became its first pastor. Laurie and I spent four days a week in Kansas City and three days a week at the farm. That arrangement seemed to work fairly well, though my interests were increasingly focused on the ministry at Heartland. I needed more time at the farm, so I began to come back to Heartland on Tuesdays. Laurie would stay in Kansas City until Thursday.

One day in Kansas City, I went into Laurie's office. She was crying. She's not a very emotional person at all. When she cries, something really big time is going on. I asked, "What in the world is the matter?"

Through her sobs, she asked, "Did you know that we're going to move to the farm?"

"Yes," I answered, "but I'm glad the Lord showed you before I had to tell you myself."

Right then, Laurie started making arrangements to move to the farm permanently. She worked diligently to tie up loose ends at the company to make the move possible, but one loose end refused to be tied: finding her own replacement as head of the agency department. Laurie had a very responsible and important position, and did a great job at it. We tried very hard to find someone to take over, but for a variety of reasons, we couldn't get a replacement. I believe this period of time was God's gift to Laurie to let her wrestle with the monumental shift of her responsibilities from Ozark to the farm and the Heartland ministry. The Lord used this time to work some things out in her, to give her more of an excitement about Heartland and prepare her for her own very significant contribution to that ministry. When she first made that commitment, it was out of sheer obedience to the Lord. Little vision . . . no joy . . . just raw obedience. After a long time of waiting and struggling, God honored her obedience by changing her heart and giving her a phenomenal ministry. But that came later. At this point, Laurie was moving to the farm and Heartland's ministry only because God told her to go.

Heartland began to take shape in the summer of 1995. We dreamed and prayed and drew sketches on paper. Soon we scheduled phases to accommodate all the growth and development we envisioned. We realized the fulfillment would take years and millions of dollars. That insight didn't frustrate us at all. We were well aware that God has His own timing and His own ways. Heartland is God's vision, not mine. We were content to follow His leading and His timetable.

We planned to have a groundbreaking ceremony in September, but we had some important business to tend to first. An old house trailer was on the slope near the lake, right in the middle of the area where we were to build all our main facilities. In this trailer, people had performed Satanic rituals. When we looked inside, we saw evidence of sacrifices. In fact, some of our calves had been stolen to sacrifice to the devil. We found the remains of a calf, and I was amazed to see incisions on that animal that looked like they would have required a skilled surgeon.

> We were well aware that God has His own timing and His own ways. Heartland is God's vision, not mine. We were content to follow His leading and His timetable.

We didn't want to proceed in fulfilling the vision God had given us without dealing appropriately with this site. We burned the trailer, then we dug a hole with a backhoe and buried it. After that, we walked all over the property and committed it to God. We pled the shed blood of Jesus Christ which overcomes the evil one, and we claimed that property back for the Lord. We prayed, "Lord, this is Yours! In Your name we cast out Satan and his demons and all their activity and dominion." This was a powerful and moving ceremony.

We were then ready for the official groundbreaking. We invited people from all over this part of the state, and about 200 people came on that September 22nd. The number of people was remarkable because the day was bitterly cold. Frost covered the ground that morning, and puddles of water froze solid. Such cold was unusual for that time of the year, but our vision for the future was unusual, too. We had a wonderful service that day. We set up a tent so people could stay warm. To symbolize the size of our vision, we didn't turn a shovel full of dirt when we broke ground; we used the backhoe to dig a hole the size of a swimming pool!

> To symbolize the size of our vision, we didn't turn a shovel full of dirt when we broke ground; we used the backhoe to dig a hole the size of a swimming pool!

I spoke for a few minutes, and I told everyone we were going to build a place for hurting people, a spiritual hospital. And I told them we guaranteed cure if people would take the medicine. That medicine is Jesus Christ.

Even before the groundbreaking, children came to us— very needy children—who were desperate for love and safety. The way we were to provide for them was to build a strong, loving community of families where truth and love are spoken clearly and lived consistently. It would be a place of protection, a place where these young people could feel loved.

That day of groundbreaking and commemoration was a great day for me. Generally, I'm not too interested in the beginning of a project. I want to see the job done, the house completed, the life changed. Yet I knew this day was special to those who shared our vision, to our northeast Missouri neighbors, and to the Lord. That was exciting to me.

We said we weren't going to take anybody's contribution to Heartland until we had put in all we had and we could show a product. Many people have great, grandiose ideas, and they want somebody else to finance it. We had a great idea, but we made a commitment to put our own money into it to make it a viable, growing ministry. After that, people who want to contribute to Heartland can be sure their money will be used wisely and effectively.

We brought the bulldozers onto the property and dug the footings for three houses where families could live and take in the needy children. I was going to build the lodge first—the camp I had originally envisioned. That's what I thought the Lord wanted me to do, but soon I realized I had misunderstood. We needed families and stability first, and we needed a school for them, too. The lodge would come later.

Of course, we needed competent, qualified, godly men and women to come to Heartland and provide leadership for each part of the ministry. Among those who were drawn to Heartland was a man who came with strong recommendations. Soon, however, I began to have second thoughts about him. He talked often about the Old Testament sacrifices—a little too often. I dismissed my misgivings about him several times, but still. . . .

One day I couldn't stand it any longer. I took the man aside and said, "Look, I've got to ask you a question. What do you believe about sacrifices? What do you believe about the blood? What do you believe about Jesus?" He looked surprised, but I continued, "I notice you keep saying things about sacrifices. Exactly what do you believe about them?"

He replied very clearly, "I believe the blood of Jesus will suffice for your past sins, but for new sin, God requires us to sacrifice animals."

I immediately replied, "Sir, the only thing that's going to be sacrificed here is you!" After a few seconds to let the shock settle down for both of us, I asked him, "Where in the world did you come up with that teaching?"

"Paul taught this perspective," he told me.

"No, sir. The apostle Paul taught very clearly that Jesus' blood is the one and only sacrifice for sin—once and for all."

He then talked about the passage in 1 Corinthians 9 where Paul had written, "To the Jews, I became like a Jew, to win the Jews. . . . I have become all things to all men so that by all possible means I might save some" (vv. 20, 22).

I replied that Paul didn't mean he was throwing away the truth of the gospel of Christ that he had lived for, suffered for, and was prepared to die for. Paul only meant that he didn't let any cultural barriers keep him from building relationships with people—so he could share the clear, life-changing truth of the gospel with them. He didn't buy my argument.

I looked him square in the eyes and said, "Look, you will have to leave Heartland. I love you, but I don't love what you believe! If you don't believe the blood of Jesus is enough, I've got a real problem, because that's what I believe!"

This man had wonderful children, and they seemed to fit in very well here, but I couldn't let someone come and preach "a different gospel." That wasn't an option. People liked this man, so I thought there may be some backlash from them when I fired him, but there was no problem at all. I guess they had the same questions and concerns I'd had about him. I found out later that a group in England promotes his belief about sacrifices. I don't know how he learned those things from them, but somehow, he did. I certainly couldn't allow someone in a responsible position here at Heartland to practice and teach cultic things.

As Heartland began, our farming operation included about 10,000 acres of pasture and grain, and a herd of about 6,500 beef cattle. Jon Simmons, our general manager, came here as a young man. He had run heavy equipment, and I saw a lot of potential in him. I said, "Jon, you don't want to run a bulldozer the rest of your life. Why don't you take this operation and run it for me?" He was very reluctant, but finally he was persuaded to join me in running the farm. I trained him to take on the role of general manager. Without Jon, I couldn't run the farm as it is today. He is much more than a co-worker; he is a faithful friend. I am very proud of him. Jon is a great blessing to me . . . a man who has earned my complete trust.

About a year after Heartland began, Jon came to me and said out of the blue, "Charlie, I think we ought to start a dairy."

When he said that, I somehow knew his idea was on target. Instantly, I said "Jon, you're right."

The Spirit was working to show Jon what we should do. I was excited because God revealed His will to Jon first, then He confirmed it to me. In the Old Testament, the Lord said, "I'll come down and put my Spirit on Moses and on other people so they can help carry this load." That's the way the Lord works today, too.

The transition from the beef business to the dairy business was painful! We knew it would take seven million dollars to build the dairy. We had spent years building a high quality beef herd. Some of those old ranchers down in Texas think theirs are the best beef cattle in the world, but they didn't think more highly of their herds than I did of mine. We were beef people through and through. We took great pride in putting out the best beef steaks money could buy. You could cut our steaks with a fork. We fed our calves fast and hard and put them on the market in twelve and thirteen months—from birth weight to

> Some of those old ranchers down in Texas think theirs are the best beef cattle in the world, but they didn't think more highly of their herds than I did of mine.

1,200 pounds. That fast rate is very unusual, but we had built them up through very carefully engineered genetics. That's why our growth rates were so phenomenal.

In spite of our commitment to beef, I knew Jon was right in suggesting we enter the dairy business. Still, I wanted to do both. I prayed, "Lord, I have a solution. We'll build a dairy, and we will have both dairy and beef."

The Lord said, "No."

So we got rid of the beef. We sold every one of our beef cattle.

God was certainly giving Jon wisdom. Soon after we made the transition to the dairy business, the beef business absolutely went in the toilet! And the dairy business is the best it has ever been. For example, in the last three years, beef has gone from eighty-five cents a pound to sixty cents. It was costing us sixty cents to produce a pound of beef. Not much margin there!

God didn't tell us to go into the pork business. Pork has gone from fifty cents a pound to fifteen cents. That would have been a disaster!

God instructed us to go into the dairy business, and we obeyed. We figure a break-even on dairy is eleven or twelve cents for a pound of milk. Today we're making eighteen cents. We think we could hold things together very well at twelve cents. God knew, and God spoke. We were just smart enough to listen.

Today we are buying a few beef cattle again. We can buy them for two hundred dollars a head less than what we got for them. It's an incredible situation when you can make two hundred dollars a head by buying your own cattle. The Lord protects and provides.

The dairy is the centerpiece of the operations at Heartland. It is the engine that makes everything else go. The dairy business provides jobs for young men in the Recovery Center and for people in the community, and it provides income to fund the entire operation. We think we can create an industry that will produce twelve million dollars a year of income with a net of two million dollars.

Our vision for Heartland has been huge from the beginning. God gave us the vision to build a church, a school, a dairy, a Recovery Center, a summer camp, a lodge, retail stores, houses, and an entire community of faith. I knew all this would require a great deal of money. I've never liked asking people for money—unless it was for an investment. I recoiled at the thought of spending my time going out and asking people for donations. If that's what God wanted me to do, I'd do it, but that sure wasn't my first choice. One day I was praying about how we would finance the incredible vision for Heartland, and the Lord spoke to me and asked, "Charlie, do you have children?"

I answered, "Yes, Lord. You know I do."

He continued, "Are they anything like you?"

"Yes, Lord. They are."

Then God said to me, "And My children are like Me. I'm a creator, and My children can create wealth to accomplish My purposes."

God never gives us a job that He doesn't provide the tools to accomplish. In some cases people need to raise money for certain projects, but in other cases God gives us the insight to build businesses to create the needed finances and also provide jobs for people. That's what God directed us to do here at Heartland. The purpose of the dairy business is to generate enough income to fund the ministry, and the added benefit is that the dairy business is a source of good jobs for many, many people. We gladly welcome willing contributions, but I don't believe God wants me to spend my time soliciting them. God has called me to spend time in prayer and the study of His Word so I will be the leader this ministry needs. He has also called me to be involved in the dairy as a source of funds and employment for our people. That calling is very clear.

Today we have about 3,000 head of dairy cows, but we plan to eventually have 10,000. As we get more cattle, we'll provide more jobs. As more jobs are available, we can have more people in the Recovery Center. And as people come here to be part of the program, they will meet Jesus Christ. He is the source of light and life; He is the one who can change lives and turn despair into hope.

> And as people come here to be part of the program, they will meet Jesus Christ. He is the source of light and life; He is the one who can change lives and turn despair into hope.

People ask about our program at the Recovery Center, and they expect a detailed analysis of psychological processes of dealing with addictions. I don't give that to them because it isn't needed. The very best psychology I've ever seen begins with people coming into a relationship with Jesus Christ to experience His cleansing and His power. Next they find intense, loving relationships in which they are held accountable for their words and actions. Finally, they learn to work hard and develop skills they can use the rest of their lives. During this process, the Holy Spirit is at work to shine the light of the Scriptures into the heart of every young person who enters the program. I tell you, it's exciting to see God at work! Christ came to save sinners, and He never intended for those sinners to stay locked in bondage to drugs, sex, pornography, stealing, or any other sin. Christ saves, and He delivers. His power can set a captive free from any sin, no matter how tight the grip might be. I know because He's done exactly that for me, and I've seen Him set many other people free as well.

It all starts with a humble acknowledgment of our deep need for a Savior. Christ came to seek and to save the lost. If we don't admit we are lost, we won't look for a Savior. Satan has deceived a lot of people in the church today. Many people believe they are Christians simply because they go to church and are involved in some religious practices. Recently a man came to one of our services at Heartland Community Church. He grew up going to church, and he believed he had done all that was required of him. I asked him, "When did you give your life to the Lord?"

He said, "I've always been in church. I've always known the Lord."

As we talked, however, I found the truth. He never knew the Lord; he had only been religious. How many people are like that? Far too many. Years ago a preacher began asking people a question to help them determine where they stood with Christ. He asked, "If you were to die today and stand before God and He asked you, 'Why should I let you into heaven?' what would you tell Him?" Many people who sit in pews on Sunday mornings would say things like, "I've lived a good life," "I've been good to people," "I've never killed anybody," or "My good deeds outweigh my bad ones." But these answers simply won't do. Our efforts may seem noble to us, but they fall far short of God's standard of perfect righteousness. Our sins deserve punishment—the punishment of death. That's exactly the price Christ paid for you and me. The only right answer to that preacher's question is: "The only reason God could let me into heaven is that I have trusted Jesus Christ's death on the cross to pay the penalty for my sins, and He has given me eternal life."

After we interviewed families to select house parents for the children who were sent here, we chose a man and his wife who had said all the right things. They said they were committed to the Lordship of Christ and they wanted to minister here at Heartland, but before long, we experienced conflict. It turned out that they wanted to minister *their* way. They didn't want any supervision at all, and they weren't open to instruction or correction. They told me they needed certain things to make them "comfortable." They were sure they had all the right solutions for any problem, and they convinced several others they were justified in their views. But in my opinion, they didn't have their focus on the children at all, and thought Heartland was going to be an easy place for them to hang out and do whatever they wanted.

I confronted them—and the lid came off! They were good house parents, but the issue was their attitude of self-sufficiency and pride. I hoped they would see this confrontation as an opportunity to repent, learn, and grow, but instead they circled the wagons! In fact, they tried to get others in our Heartland community to join them inside their circle. Several other families got confused: they listened to them and felt they were right, then they'd listen to me and felt I was right. Finally, this couple's hard heart forced me to ask them to leave. They had stronger relationships with others than the sacrifice-focused man had, so this situation caused far more heartache, confusion, and despair. It took months for those of us who stayed behind to sort things out and learn to trust each other again.

They were tests to see how we would handle them, and they were God's training seminars to equip us to follow Him more closely.

It would be nice if God followed every vision with a smooth path to accomplish it, but His plan involves people, and people are often difficult! Satan's desire is for problems to get us off track and destroy the hope God has put in us. God allows difficulties for a completely different reason: to help us grow stronger. These problems weren't surprises to God. They were tests to see how we would handle them, and they were God's training seminars to equip us to follow Him more closely.

We haven't had many difficult people like this couple and the man who believed the sacrificial system was still valid. In fact, some wonderful couples have joined us at Heartland. They have left positions at schools, businesses, and farms to come and be a part of what God is doing with us. Their commitment to the Lord is demonstrated in their love for each other, their hard work, their strong prayer life, and their genuine care for the children who come into our ministry. Some of these people are house parents. Their consistent love and discipline provides a godly environment for young hearts to experience love, young minds to learn truth, and young bodies to grow strong. Others have joined us at the school or in the dairy. Their efforts, too, are an integral part of the integrated vision of the school, the Recovery Center, the church, and a profitable dairy which helps fund the entire operation.

Most of the couples who are attracted to Heartland come because they identify with our strong sense of community and our desire to minister to hurting kids. Some of these couples come from middle-income situations, so the prospect of moving into a new, spacious home is very attractive to them. Many are wonderful people who work hard to make everyone's dream a reality. Sadly, a few prefer a handout to hard work. They see themselves as needy as the children, and they want to be first in line to receive help. Certainly all of us need help, but couples who become house parents need to be strong enough and mature

HEARTLAND CHRISTIAN ACADEMY

enough to get their eyes off themselves and onto the needs of the children. God has His hand on this ministry, and He gets involved when people don't fit His purpose. He uses the chisel of confrontation and the sandpaper of high expectations to shape people's characters. If they are willing, God gladly changes them and helps them grow. If they are unwilling, however, they don't last long here. Our work is far too important—kids' lives are far too precious—to have selfish or apathetic people care for them.

Our standards for house parents are extremely—and necessarily—high. For the sake of these children, we can accept only godly, mature couples as models for them. Couples who aren't yet qualified for that role can find a position in the dairy, working the land, or in some other important job. Over time, they may grow and become qualified to be house parents. In the meantime, they can soak up the love of God and the truth of His Word as they are active in our fellowship.

I started buying land in 1965 as Ozark began prospering. Years later, I was able to buy my father's land. One principle I have lived by is to never ask anyone to sell me their land. Land is a sacred, family possession. It's simply not right to pursue property that may have been in a family for generations. People know I am interested in land. If they want to sell, they come to me and I'll buy it. If not, I won't. It's that simple.

In the late 80s, we had about five or six thousand acres, and we got into the beef cattle business in a big way. Today we have about sixteen thousand acres. I never had any intentions of having this much land, but we use it. We farm it so it will be productive, and we improve it so it can be even more productive.

Farming is a very difficult business. Over the years, I have often scratched my head wondering why we worked so hard to farm, yet made so little money. Now I know why the Lord led us to acquire this land and build a farm: so He could provide jobs and stability for young people in our program at Heartland. All along, this has been God's plan.

When we have a problem here at Heartland, we address it clearly and lovingly. After all, that's what God does with us. But God is also incredibly patient, and I try to follow His example in that way, too. I very seldom give up on somebody. If people demonstrate a willing, teachable spirit, I'm willing to give them plenty of time to change and develop. People seem to appreciate that kind of encouragement and patience, and many of them use that opportunity to grow strong in the Lord and develop new habits of diligence and hard work that will pay dividends for the rest of their lives.

When Laurie and I moved here permanently, we appreciated the sense of purpose in each family and individual at Heartland. We have a new depth of trust in our relationships with the people here that can only be built by living among them. We see each other every day in every conceivable situation, and we interact about the most profound as well as the most trivial issues in life. We work together, play together, and worship together. We depend on each other, and we know we can count on the strength and wisdom we see in one another when the going is tough.

Several years ago, a young couple, Michael and Ruth Bevis, prepared to go to Malaysia with Asian Ministry Teams of the Ervin Rutherford mission group. As I talked to them, I sensed this wasn't the best course for them to take. I said, "Michael, you're not ready to go. I think you should stay in the United States for a while and grow so you'll be better prepared." With a firm commitment to serve the Lord, however, Michael and Ruth determined to go.

Even though I didn't think the Bevises were prepared spiritually and emotionally to go overseas, I tried to help them any way I could. I bought their car, and I loaned them some money they needed. I thought, *They'll make some mistakes along the way and realize they're making a mistake, but they will learn a lot by going. And who knows, maybe they'll make it work.*

Michael and Ruth arrived in Malaysia, but after a few months they came home and moved to Springfield, Missouri. We contacted Michael to see if he and Ruth wanted to come to Heartland. He said, "Yes." They were eager to join us. I am so glad they came! This young couple has added so much to our family of faith. I didn't believe they were ready to go to Malaysia, but I was sure they were ready to come to Heartland. Michael is the principal of our school, and they are both involved on our worship team. Michael is the leader of the worship team, and he does a fantastic job. They both have great gifts and skills, and they are using them powerfully in this ministry. I trust this is a good place for them to grow. Perhaps God is preparing them to go back to Malaysia or some other spot overseas. We'll see. But for now, I'm very glad this fine young couple is ministering at Heartland.

In the months after the school started, we received call after call from parents and pastors who needed a place to send young men who had drug and alcohol problems. Many of these young men, of course, also had criminal records. At first, we didn't have a place that fit this need, but as the calls kept coming, we quickly realized that God wanted us to provide a loving, stable environment for them. That's how the Recovery Center began . . . out of necessity.

At the time, Heartland Community Church was meeting in a building next to the land and cattle office. When the school building was finished, we moved our church services into the school and freed up a big, spacious place. We had to work hard to put partitions in it so it could be used as the men's Recovery Center. Greg Baust, an Australian, came to Heartland to run the program at the center. Under his leadership, we made good progress. The center combined a strong sense of accountability with hard, consistent work and a bold commitment to Jesus Christ. Over half of the young men who came into the program during those first years made dramatic progress. I wish I could say all of them improved, but they didn't. Baust told a reporter for the Kansas City Star, "The government feels you're doing well if you can help four percent. We want to do a lot better than that." The young men who come into our program range in age from fourteen to thirty-five. Of course, if they are of school age, they attend Heartland school in addition to working. If they have graduated from high school, they work full time on the farm.

Greg did great work getting our center going. Young men learned to turn away from easy—and destructive— answers to their problems, and they began to acquire lifelong habits of trusting God, depending on His Word, and working hard to earn a living. Greg's vision for the Recovery Center was to keep it small to be sure to give adequate attention to everyone involved. He wanted us to remain at about ten young men. I believed, however, that the number of calls we were receiving were signals from God that if we grew, God would send us all the help we needed.

One of those who came to us in those first years was Ron Osbon, from Kahoka, Missouri. By the time Ron was eighteen years old, he was in jail for burglary and drug possession. He was paroled so he could come to Heartland and participate in the program at the Recovery Center. Since he had graduated from high school, Ron was able to devote ten hours a day, six days a week to working cattle. With everyone else in the program, he attended a Bible class every morning at 7 o'clock. The Sunday schedule included Sunday school and two worship services, morning and evening.

Ron commented, "It's given me more responsibility. It keeps me busy, out of trouble. If you talk to my parents, they'll tell you I'm a completely different person now."

My grandson, Rob Patchin, was working at the farm when we began the Recovery Center, and he offered to help some evenings. Soon, God used him profoundly in the lives of these young men, and he sensed God's calling to be more involved. He talked to me about his desires, and I was thrilled that he wanted God to use him in this way. We worked out a schedule so he could spend half his time on the farm and half at the Recovery Center.

In the second year of the Recovery Center, I noticed that Greg was looking tired, and his fatigue continued for several months. I wondered if he was getting enough sleep, but that didn't seem to be the problem. Then God gave me some insight. I asked him, "Greg, do you know why you're tired?"

"No," he answered, "I can't figure it out."

"I think you're frustrated. Frustration will tire you out faster than anything in the world. You're not tired because of your work. I think you're tired because you're frustrated. That kind of fatigue is like a short circuit in a battery. When you use your energy for yourself, it tires you out. When you use your energy for others, you gain energy. It's like the bunny in the battery commercial: it just keeps going and going."

Greg looked as if he understood, but nothing changed as days and weeks went by. After a few more months, Greg left our ministry and I asked Rob to take over. He has done a wonderful job there shepherding the other staff and leading the program. Rob knows how to pray. That makes a tremendous difference. I can spot that difference in people in a second—one who prays and one who doesn't. One person is running on empty, and the other is running on the spiritual power and direction of the Lord. Rob brings maturity, spiritual power, and prayer to the leadership role at the Recovery Center. He's doing a terrific job.

In the thirty years I was out of the church, a very strange thing took place in the church in America. The level of knowledge increased a great deal, but the degree of spirituality severely declined. Today we have knowledge, but that knowledge is not being converted into faith, hope, and love. For example, go to a Christian bookstore today and look around. The shelves are filled with wonderful, insightful books written by highly educated and gifted authors, but these insights don't seem to be affecting the rates of divorce, teen pregnancy, abortions, and drug abuse among those calling themselves Christians. Thirty years ago, very few people, and even fewer Christians, experienced these tragedies. Today, they affect the church at just about the same level as exists in the non-Christian world. Now that, my friend, is a real tragedy.

Several times a week someone calls to find out how to get a young person into the Recovery Center, and almost every week we have parents visit who want to check us out before entrusting their teenager to us for a year. How do they hear about us? I honestly don't know, but it's amazing. People hear about our program, and they hear about our successes, and they want to know more. When one person finds a good thing, he tells others about it. I suppose that's how people from all over the country find out about Heartland. We've never spent a dime on advertising. We haven't needed to. People we know—and people we don't know—do our marketing for us for free.

One of the signs that tells me we are making a difference in the lives of young people is that several of them have joined our staff after completing their program. One of our staff members came here after I went to a jail to get him out. He entered the program, and God touched his life. He's been here about two and one-half years, and is a phenomenal leader at the Recovery Center. Have any of them been in trouble with the law? So has he. Have any of them been hooked on drugs? He can identify with them. Have any of them felt hopeless? He has, too. Do any of them have trouble learning to be disciplined and work hard? Yes, he went through that phase when he started. Do any of them have just a glimmer of hope that God can change their lives and give them meaning, purpose, and strength? He knows all it takes is that glimmer. A little hope and a big God can do a lot in a person's life.

> We've never spent a dime on advertising. We haven't needed to. People we know—and people we don't know—do our marketing for us for free.

Another sign of success is when someone in our program becomes a soul-winner. One Sunday morning I invited people to respond to Christ's gracious offer of forgiveness. A tall, slender young man in his thirties—a friend of a former drug addict who had gone through our program—came forward. This tall stranger was trusting in

Christ because a former drug addict had become an evangelist. One person's life and words had been touched by God while in our Recovery Center, and now his life and his words were touching someone else. I believe that is success!

We ask the young men and their parents to sign a one-year commitment to the program. We have found that it takes at least that long for their habits and lifestyles to change. That year is truly a life-changing experience for most people. They develop new habits and new, deep friendships based on trust and love rather than empty manipulation. By the end of that year, many of them don't want to leave. In some cases, they want to stay because they know the pitfalls of the life they came from, and they are rightfully afraid of slipping back into those sins. We want to prepare them so they will be strong enough and wise enough to make good decisions when they return home. And we make sure they understand the importance of finding a solid, loving, supportive fellowship of believers.

The schedule at the Recovery Center is very regimented. These young men desperately need the stability that a disciplined schedule and high expectations can provide. Rob is an ex-Marine. He runs the Center like boot camp, and the participants love him because they are sure he cares for them. He has great compassion, and he demonstrates it in a thousand ways to these young men.

They get up early in the morning and have devotions led by Rob or his staff. Many of these young men have been to school, of course, but some are seventeen years old and haven't progressed past their freshman courses due to truancy. At that rate they will never graduate, so we help them get a G.E.D. If they get their G.E.D. and a driver's license, and if they trust in Christ and grow strong in Him, and if we teach them how to work and earn a living—we've made some important changes in their lives! If they were to trust Christ but they didn't know how to work, how would they make it when they leave Heartland? Show me a man who doesn't know how to work, and I'll show you a person whose entire life is a wreck. Faith and discipline to work go hand in hand.

The biggest struggle in seeing this vision grow is finding people who have a servant's heart. That may sound simple, but we live in an age of narcissism. Some people think that the most important quality in people is their level of skills, but skills can be taught. The quality that is by far the most important is *heart*. People can be taught to *do*, but they can't be taught to *care*. A person's true character doesn't surface immediately. It is revealed only after it is tested and exposed. People can talk about how much they want to serve God and obey Him, but their hearts are revealed when hours of ministry are long, people don't respond to their care, and they face other hardships. I don't think people intentionally lie and say they want to serve when they actually don't. Many of them want to do what is right. They simply haven't had those desires refined and strengthened through adversity.

We typically avoid adversity at all costs, but we should embrace it because we can learn so much from it. A humble, servant spirit is more valuable than gold. Many of our people here at Heartland make us rich with that kind of selfless lifestyle, and others are being tested and refined so they can acquire it.

The future of Heartland is bright and big. Five years from now, I want to have a convention center which will be a gathering place for people of every tribe, tongue, and nation to grow in their faith and to sharpen their ministry skills. This convention center will include two hundred hotel rooms and a free-standing restaurant. The center will be a haven for missionaries who are returning from overseas and need a rest, and it will be a launching pad for those who are about to go. I believe many different organizations will use that facility to further their ministries. We will welcome all who are dedicated to the lordship of Christ and the salvation of the lost.

We want to put in a supermarket at Heartland within five years to serve the growing community, and we will probably add several retail shops selling all kinds of things. Before long, Heartland will become a free-standing community of three to four thousand. That kind of growth will take ten years or so. I want to bring in products and services our people can afford. I want to get good quality material at good prices. We can control which stores open because it's our land. We don't have to let a store open at Heartland if the goods they sell or the way they sell them aren't consistent with our values. In other words, if somebody wants to sell pornography or other kinds of trash, they will have to find some other place to locate that store.

As our dairy operation grows, we plan to expand and build a processing plant for milk and milk products. We'll develop our own retail chain and sell milk products under our own label. The driving purpose of everything is to glorify the Lord. If we grow, it will be because growth will allow us to glorify God more. If growth can't accomplish that purpose, then we won't pursue expansion at all. I want our business interests not only to provide financial resources and jobs for our ministry here at Heartland; I want us to have an impact for Christ on the business world. I hope people who do business with us will say, "There's something about those people. They have integrity and they really care about people. I want what they have."

Today many Christians are afraid to speak out about Christ in business and politics. A few in the vocal minority against God have put that fear in us, and it's a shame. We need to speak out boldly about our Savior to everyone who will listen. And we also need to back up those words with a lifestyle that demonstrates the love and power of Jesus Christ. People who love Jesus and act with integrity and kindness stick out like sore thumbs . . . and like lights in the world.

Again, one of our biggest obstacles to expansion is finding godly men and women to spearhead different aspects of growth. Too often, people depend on their own experiences and push their own agendas instead of depending on Christ and seeking His will. At Heartland there is no distinction between business and ministry. Everything we do is to glorify God, and every aspect must be guided by the Holy Spirit and achieved by God's grace and power. People may say, "Well, Charlie, this is your vision and you're running the show." That's not the case at all. A man seventy-one years old doesn't suddenly get a bright idea about building a Christian community in northeast Missouri! This is God's vision, His plan, and it is up to Him to make it happen. I'm just doing what the Lord is telling me to do.

> People who love Jesus and act with integrity and kindness stick out like sore thumbs . . . and like lights in the world.

All of us have mixed motives. As people come to Heartland and get involved, the Lord will reveal to them any selfish desires and prideful agendas. At each point of their training, they can repent, trust Christ for cleansing, and choose to serve Him instead of themselves. However, they can also choose to harden their hearts to the Holy Spirit's convicting work. They may become withdrawn; they may become angry; they may run.

Recently a man came to Heartland and began working in our dairy. After being here for a while, the Lord showed him that although he had been very religious all his life, he didn't yet have a genuine relationship with God. At that point of insight, he could have hardened himself and said, "I've lived this way all my life. I'm doing just fine. There's no need to change now." In many cases, our natural inclination is to push aside the leading of the Spirit and continue to rely on our pride. But this man said, "I want to face up to what God is showing me. I've lived under an illusion all my life about religion and spirituality, but the fact is, I don't know the Lord!" That kind of admission takes courage. He initially came to Heartland saying, "I want to help," but after the Spirit convicted him, he realized he was the one needing help. I respect his honesty. God honored that honesty, and this man was born again. He told our congregation, "I came here to be a blessing, but I've been blessed. Now, I *can* be a blessing to others."

God works in the hearts of every person who joins us here at Heartland. Some realize their need for a Savior; most are convicted of some hidden, selfish desires. In any case, God graciously shows them the truth about themselves so they can repent and experience His incredible love and power in a new, rich, deep way. In all this, the Lord gives us a passion to serve Him with all our hearts. As we rub shoulders with others who love Christ with all their hearts and will follow Him anywhere, the passion for love and service is infectious. We all catch it! Almost every month someone tells me, "When I first came here, I thought I was serving God, but I was just hanging out! Now I realize what it means to have an ambition to please God."

People come to this conclusion because it's our life here: We eat it, breathe it, and sleep with it. We get up with it, and go to bed with it. We go to school or work with it, and we go home with it. We never get away from it because the

HEARTLAND COMMUNITY CHURCH

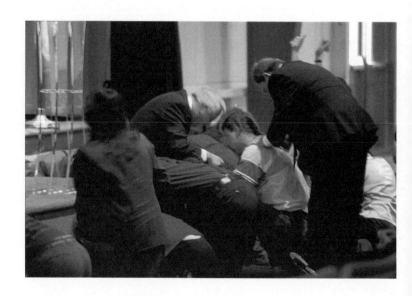

Spirit of God is in everything we do and everything we are here at Heartland. This is our commitment. It's our life.

Soon after Laurie and I moved to Heartland, God laid it on our hearts to open our home to teenage girls who need a place of love and safety. One day a woman brought her daughter here to stay, but we had a hard time finding the right home for her. Laurie turned to me and asked, "Why don't we take her?" And we did. This girl moved in, and my wife who had cried because she didn't want to come to Heartland became a house parent to a needy teenager. This woman who had never had children before suddenly had an instant family. Laurie's heart was growing, and her ministry was growing—quickly! More girls came, and now we have four. Recently Laurie looked at me and said, "I believe we could take eight. We could make room. Let's do it." She has a real vision for God using us in this way!

More than anything else, I'm praying the Lord will give us the right house parents who will provide love and stability and raise our young people according to the Bible. The Scriptures tell us exactly how to raise kids, but most people—even Christian parents—don't even read it to find out. They know the Bible speaks clearly about salvation, and they know it says a lot about the need for integrity in a person's personal life and business dealings. But most people have little idea what the Bible teaches about how to raise a child or teenager. At Heartland, we have high standards for young people. The combination of love, respect, accountability, and discipline works wonders in their hearts! The truth of God's Word is not to be heard only on Sunday morning. Moses told the children of Israel that they needed to speak and live God's truth in every situation and at every time of day. He said,

> These commandments that I give you today are to be upon your hearts. Impress them on your children. Talk about them when you sit at home and when you walk along the road, when you lie down and when you get up. Tie them as symbols on your hands and bind them on your foreheads. Write them on the doorframes of your houses and on your gates. (Deuteronomy 6:6-9)

We also believe it is very important to teach young people to respect and honor their parents. This, as most people are aware, is one of the Ten Commandments:

> Honor your father and your mother, so that you may live long in the land the Lord your God is giving you. (Exodus 20:12)

This is the first commandment accompanied with a promise, so we can be sure what the blessing will be if we obey. Notice it doesn't say we have to agree with our parents, and it doesn't say we can't have reasonable discussions with them. The passage means, however, that after the discussions, we respect our parents' decisions. This structure builds an atmosphere of trust and accountability which

RECOVERY CENTER

results in wiser decisions and healthier choices, and in turn, we experience more peace and a longer life.

Obedience has very tangible results in the life of a believer—even a young believer. In our culture, many people believe that parental authority is harsh and repressive, and they cite instances of abuse to bolster their case. Parental authority is designed by God for several important reasons: for protection, to provide good examples, and to train the young person to make good decisions. Our culture, however, values "rights" instead of wisdom. Many parents today let their children run the house. They indulge their kids with all kinds of privileges, and they make almost no demands on them to contribute to the household in any meaningful way. This "hands off" policy appears laudable in some circles, but it undermines the young person's sense of identity as a loved, contributing family member. It eliminates needed controls on their behavior, and it destroys the accountability necessary for protection and development.

> Parental authority is designed by God for several important reasons: for protection, to provide good examples, and to train the young person to make good decisions.

I believe this approach is actually destructive to these young people and their futures. The "hands off" approach is designed to avoid confrontation, but many of those who avoid conflict also avoid expressing affection. Parents are relatively uninvolved in the lives of their children, and their children are out of control, so instead of communicating affirmation, the parents always communicate frustration. That isn't love. It is anarchy.

A familiar Bible passage about parenting carries profound meaning. Solomon wrote:

> Train a child in the way he should go,
> and when he is old he will not turn from it.
> (Proverbs 22:6)

Any kind of training—boot camp for soldiers, computer skills for office workers, job skills for plumbers, or life skills for children—requires time, attention, and know-how. The training of a young life entrusted to us by God is the most sacred and important responsibility of our lives. We are to give it all we have, and trust God to build character deep into that precious young heart.

Bible scholars tell us that to train a child "in the way he should go" means the parent is to be a student of the child's gifts and talents, encouraging and confirming those special abilities. For example, if a child is gifted musically, the parents should provide opportunities for this talent to be developed—even if neither of the parents can carry a tune in a bucket! Affirming a child's talents that are very different than ours can be a challenge. In many cases, parents want (and expect) the child to grow up "just like me." If that reference is to high moral character and love for Christ, that's great! But if it refers to interests and skills, it can be devastating.

I know of a young man whose father is a college football coach. This young man, however, has no athletic talent whatsoever. He loves to work on computers and design software. During his childhood, he felt constant tension—and tremendous disapproval—from his father. He tried to play all kinds of sports when he was a little boy, but he failed miserably. Finally, after he graduated from college, his father accepted the fact that his son was not going to be the star athlete he had always dreamed he would become. But by that time almost twenty years of their relationship had been filled with scowls, grimaces, and disapproval rather than affirmation and acceptance. Training a child must blend both the authority to supervise and the wisdom to affirm the individual talents of each child.

Another deception in today's culture is that parents and children are equals, so they should relate as "buddies." Certainly there should be plenty of laughter and fun, but God instituted the family for a purpose: to train each new generation of sinners in the ways of God.

When it comes to moral standards and spiritual commitments, who are the instructors for our children? The public school system? No. Neighborhood kids? No. The church? Yes, to some degree. Yet the primary instructors for each generation of young people must be their own parents. Far too many parents abdicate that God-given privilege and responsibility, and the damage caused by this abdication is only too evident in violence, out of wedlock pregnancies, drug abuse, hopelessness, and rage. The children aren't the primary problem. Their parents' laissez faire attitudes and inaction are the problem. God help the next generation when this current generation of young people take on the role of parenthood!

Left to our human nature, we have a tendency to settle for the lowest and the least instead of the highest and the best. In addition, we segment our lives between the sacred and the secular. In our minds, we have a compartment for worshiping God on Sunday morning, but we leave Him out of the rest of the week. Some of us have a slightly larger compartment for God. We set aside time for Him every morning or evening in addition to Sunday morning, but we seldom think of Him, depend on Him, and thank Him during the rest of the day. But Jesus Christ is our Lord all day, every day. He is the source of wisdom, truth, and strength at every minute, not just during some designated hour.

Many years ago, Brother Lawrence wrote a book called *Practicing the Presence of God*. In this outstanding book, he shows how we can be aware of God's presence twenty-four hours a day, seven days a week. He describes his process of learning to be aware of God even when he washed dishes. Every activity we do is a spiritual exercise for a spiritual person. As we are aware of our need for God and His sufficiency to provide for our every need, then everything we do is in the strength of God and for the glory of God. "Lordship" means we are not our own; we have been bought with a price. We belong to another, and we live to please Him.

FARM AND DAIRY

One of the best activities for young people at Heartland is to go down to the dairy and milk cows. This regular activity builds up our ability to concentrate. Our society has been brainwashed by the way we watch television. Our minds become numb; we are almost completely passive. We even need the producers of the programs to add a laugh track so we'll know when to laugh. We just sit and soak. Many of us have lost the ability to think, make decisions, and dream dreams. We live in an age of entertainment, but many of our young people and adults are bored to death.

I've never been bored. When I was a child, I didn't have television and video games. We didn't even have a daily newspaper. We had the radio and the weekly paper—which didn't even have comics—but I never remember being bored. I was creating and thinking. When I wasn't working, I was thinking up fun things to do, and then we'd get busy doing them. We didn't sit around; we built things, played games, and stimulated our minds. Boredom wasn't a word we ever used because it was never a reality in our lives.

The lordship of Christ requires us to be active, not passive; to be alert and aware of His Spirit's prompting so we can take action, not sitting like blobs. Many of us think the entertainment of television and movies are exciting, but let me tell you, there is nothing more exciting than walking hand in hand with the King of the universe and being invited to participate in His heart, His ways, and His goals. That's real life!

Today we often hear people say: "Just do the best you can." This statement sounds good and sincere. After all, even the angels can do only their best every day! But the focus of that statement is on man, not God. It's like making a New Year's resolution to change ourselves by trying a little harder. God, however, hasn't called us to do our best in our own strength and wisdom. He has commissioned us to call on His power, His Spirit, and His grace to enable us to accomplish kingdom purposes. That's a lot bigger and better than "doing the best we can."

> There is nothing more exciting than walking hand in hand with the King of the universe and being invited to participate in His heart, His ways, and His goals. That's real life!

A lot of Christians are depressed about going to church because they go only out of duty. They've never known the joy of submitting to the lordship of Christ. They may have accepted Christ as their Savior, but they haven't taken the next step of acknowledging that they belong to Him and receiving the most exciting life they can possibly imagine. Living in their own power and for their own purposes, they live frustrated lives that are shallow and empty. They may be the seed sown on rocky soil, whose faith quickly withers and dies. The only times I feel down and despondent these days is when I have to leave my prayer time. I enjoy that time with God so much that I just don't want to leave. The solution, of course, is to take that awareness of His presence with me throughout the day and enjoy Him.

My Savior cares about even the most minute details of my life—even the white hairs on my head—and He is in charge of every aspect of my life: schedule, emotions, goals, reactions to people and situations. He has proven His love for me. I can't miss it! And I want to bless Him and please Him in every way I possibly can. I want to sense His smile.

So many times over the years, I have asked for the Lord's blessings, but recently I have begun saying, "Lord, I want to bless You." I am realizing that the greatest blessing He has given me is His presence, allowing me to experience total fulfillment and joy. As I am focused on blessing Him, my mind is clearer and my heart is alert. It's almost like being in the military when they put their forces on high alert in the face of eminent danger. The commanders give the troops live ammunition; they fuel the equipment; everything is ready for instant action. In five minutes, the planes can be in the air and the tanks can be rolling. When I am in tune with the Lord, I, too, am in a state of high alert, ready to do whatever my Heavenly Commander asks at a moment's notice.

Many Christians are in a different mode. They are in "beta." That term refers to the props on a plane when they are neither pulling nor pushing. They are turning in the wind, but they aren't productive at all. Many of us are exactly the same way. I've certainly had times when I looked good, but I wasn't doing anything significant. All the elements were there, but the power wasn't connected. It's a sad thing when believers are in "beta." God has provided power, direction, and encouragement. He has given us the most challenging and rewarding goal possible: to represent Him and advance His kingdom. But we have to acknowledge our dependence on Him and submit to His care and leading in order to tap into that power and direction. In John 15:5, Jesus said,

> I am the vine; you are the branches. If a man remains in Me and I in him, he will bear much fruit; apart from Me you can do nothing.

The power to bear fruit doesn't come by mechanically flipping a spiritual switch. It comes by being deeply involved in a rich relationship with Christ. As we know and love Him, He guides us and gives us opportunities to serve Him.

Another picture of lordship is found in the Book of Exodus. In chapter 21, Moses describes the relationship and conditions of indentured servitude, becoming a slave in order to pay off debts. He says that a man shall go free after seven years of service, but at that point, the slave has a choice:

> But if the servant declares, "I love my master . . . and do not want to go free," then his master must take him before the judges. He shall take him to the door or the doorpost and pierce his ear with an awl. Then he will be his servant for life. (Exodus 21: 5-6)

Because he loves his master, the freed slave chooses to stay and become a "bond slave." As a sign of this commitment, he has his ear pierced with an awl so everyone will know of this special, loved-based relationship. This is a picture of our relationship with Christ. We have been set free, but because we love our Master, we choose to remain in loyal service to Him. In many of his letters, the apostle Paul called himself a "bond slave of Jesus Christ." His obedience was out of his love *for* God in response to the love *of* God.

Every person is a slave of something. We don't have a choice to decide if we will be slaves, but we do get to pick our master. We may be a slave of greed, lust, entertainment, food, power, sex, alcohol, or a person. Or we can be slaves of Jesus Christ. Only one of these is a loving Master who cares about us. The others only destroy us. I've chosen to be a slave of Jesus Christ. At one point years ago I came to the same conclusion as the Prodigal Son as he fed pigs far away from home: "My father has servants who are far better off than I am." That revelation helped turn me around to go home to my Father.

> Every person is a slave of something. We don't have a choice to decide if we will be slaves, but we do get to pick our master.

I try to keep the mission of Heartland in front of our employees at our quarterly dinners so they will feel a sense of ownership in the ministry there. I want them to know that this is just as much their ministry as it is mine and Laurie's.

Rob Patchin

—Director of the
Recovery Center

I started helping
Greg Baust, the first
director of the Recov-
ery Center, soon after
it began several years
ago. I was working a
full-time job here on
the farm as the feed manager, but I wanted to be a
part of what they were doing, so I took guys to town
and ran errands for them when they needed me.
Soon I felt the Lord wanted me to be even more involved with the Recovery Center, so I split my time
half and half between the Center and the farm. I really enjoyed being a part of God's work with these
men as they trusted Christ to change their lives.

Years later, in January of 1998, Greg left his position, and there was a need for a replacement. I
guess I was in the right place at the right time. I believe God has called me to be a pastor to these young
men as well as a pastor at Heartland Community
Church. Right now, God has me responsible for the

Recovery Center. I'll do that until He calls me to do something else.

Our purpose at the Recovery Center is to help these young men not only find Jesus but also become grounded and solidified in their faith. Their backgrounds are in drugs, alcohol, gangs . . . you name it, and they had very few real commitments before they came here. When things start getting tough, they simply quit and did something that was easier. That doesn't work here at the Recovery Center. We want to instill in them a "stick-to-it-iveness" so they can follow through with their commitments, no matter what. Each of these young men makes a one-year commitment. It's not legally binding, but we take a man at his word. If they decide to leave before the year is finished, we remind them of their commitment to stay.

We believe it takes at least a year—maybe even two years—to change the heart of a man so he'll be ready to make it on his own. During the first month the young men are here, they have to go through the most important transition. Some of those who come are in their 20s and 30s. They come because they realize they are at the end of their ropes. They have been out on their own, but they haven't been making it. Their transition during that first month is relatively easy. The teenagers, however, have more of a struggle because they are leaving their moms and dads. They may not have been getting along with their parents, but being away from them is traumatic. They feel homesick, and many of the teenagers want to leave in those first weeks. For this reason, we don't let them have contact with their parents for the first month. Before we had this rule, we saw kids lay a heavy guilt trip on their parents for putting them in the Recovery Center. The teenagers complained, "You won't believe what they're doing to me here! They expect me to work . . . and to study! You've got to get me out of this place!" Of course, this is exactly what the parents and the teenagers knew the program would require of them, but reality is sometimes hard to take. On a few occasions, these parents couldn't stay strong. They were manipulated by the guilt, and the process of change broke down. We are committed to tough love, hard work, and sound studies, but manipulation and guilt can undermine those positive qualities. That's the reason we instituted the one-month no contact period. After that, the vast majority of young people make friends and feel much more comfortable. If we take away their access to manipulate their parents for a short while, they have a much greater chance of success. This is the most significant time in the program.

The Bible talks about the difference between "the narrow way" and "the broad way." I was reading that passage not long ago, and it struck me that the narrow way takes sacrifice. The broad way, the way that leads to hell, doesn't require sacrifice, commitment, and obedience. It's easier, but it's deadly. We communicate to these men and young people in the Recovery Center that there are costs in following the narrow way of obedience to Christ, but there are incredible benefits, too. In many ways, that's one of the biggest lessons we teach and model here: the benefits of making the daily, difficult choices to follow Jesus.

I could tell a lot of terrific stories about how God has changed lives through the Recovery Center. I'd like to relate one or two of them. One young man, Will, came here about fourteen months ago. He's nineteen years old. He grew up in a Christian home, but his parents spoiled him. They seldom asked him to do anything difficult, and they gave him whatever he wanted. Will is a very bright young man, but he used his intelligence to commit credit card fraud. The police finally caught him, and after his trial he was released to come here. Will had never worked a day in his life, so farm work was really hard for him. In those first few weeks, if he worked four hours a day, he slept fourteen hours! As time went on, he became a good worker.

About six or eight months into the program, Will made friends with a young man who really struggled here. One night I caught Will and this guy smoking marijuana behind the barn. I told him, "Will, you know our policy. I'm going to have to let you go.

But after thirty days, you can come back if you want to."

I felt strongly that Will would come back. He had made such remarkable progress, and I thought he wouldn't let this keep him from continuing it. I sure wanted him to come back, and I prayed that he would. Will's parents told him that he couldn't come back home. I was pleasantly surprised with their decision. They were through pampering him. That, too, was a turning point for Will. He would have to make it on his own.

Will had saved over $1,000 while he was working here on the farm, so he went to a town near Heartland and rented a room for a month. He got cable television, and he ate pizza almost every meal for that thirty days. By the end of that time, Will was out of money, but he wasn't out of hope. He called me and said, "Rob, I want to come back to Heartland."

Since Will has been back, he's made a lot of progress. He's had some ups and downs, but that's expected of all our young people. He's doing really well. When we came back, he knew he had to start over. He had spent almost eight months with us, but he was starting over from scratch. Including his month of pizza sabbatical, he will have been here a year and nine months. He's the cook at the Center right now, and he's doing a great job with that responsibility. Will's success story isn't finished, but the chapters are being written every day.

In another wonderful story, one of the first young men in our program is now the youth pastor at Heartland Community Church. Ron Osbon came to the Recovery Center in the spring of 1996. Ron had been heavily involved in drugs, and he faced fourteen years in prison for breaking and entering. The judge gave him five years probation instead of prison time so he could come to Heartland and enter the Recovery Center. Ron became a Christian soon after he came to us. After he graduated from our program, Ron grew in the Lord in incredible ways. He is a faithful and godly young man. Now he works with me side by side here at the Center, as well as serving as one our youth leaders. God has called him to be a pastor, and he's already fulfilling it.

All of us have some bumpy times. I like to compare our lives to a river. The rocks and boulders in the river are the difficulties and tests we face, and the water is our spirituality. The more water we have in our river, the smoother the ride. The rocks are still there, but they won't knock holes in the boat or swamp us if the water is high enough. On a number of occasions early in his time here, Ron's water got low and he struggled. That seldom happens today. His river runs deep.

Mark Owens was the very first person in our program. He was on drugs for years, and he could have been put in prison for many years for shipping drugs through the mail. When he came to us, he realized that he desperately needed accountability so his life would change. Mark responded. God changed his life. He's now an integral part of our church. That's a great story of God's mercy in Mark's life . . . and in my life as I've been able to watch Mark walk with Jesus.

Accountability is a hallmark of our program. We don't have a psychologist running the Recovery Center. We use the basic tools of discipleship in providing love, honesty, and accountability to help people follow through with their commitments to change and follow Christ. We talk about Jesus' love and strength, and we try to model the love He has for these men. In that environment, God works His miracles in their lives.

In the next few years, I expect our ministry at the Center to double or triple. We have people call us from all over the country right now. I don't have a clue how they heard about us, but they call seeking help. In the future, we'll have to expand to fill the growing needs. We are now networking with a few other centers which have shorter programs, and men come here who need love, truth, and accountability for a longer period of time.

As we grow, we'll need additional competent staff. My granddad and I believe most of these staff will be people who have been in our program. As their lives are changed, they will want to share those experiences with others. God will send some from other centers, but most will be homegrown.

Sometimes it's hard for me to believe that God would be so gracious to allow me to be a part of His work in people's lives at the Recovery Center. I am so unworthy, but God has called me to love them and minister to them. God has strengthened me as I have watched Him work through me. Our family has been strengthened, too. Our whole family is committed to seeing God work through us, and that's very encouraging to me. I want to thank my wife Carin for her support and love. She has helped me be what I am today. Sometimes I feel like there's not enough time in the day to fulfill all my responsibilities at the Recovery Center and at home, but God gives strength.

JON SIMMONS

—General Manager of
Sharpe Land & Cattle
Company

In the early 80s,
Charlie hired my dad
and me to build levies
with bulldozers on his land. We worked there for
about three months, and Charlie told me a number
of times, "Jon, you're going to come work for me
full-time." I laughed the first few times, but Charlie
didn't stop asking me to manage construction on his
farm.

Over those three months, I watched Charlie very
carefully. I saw that he was successful, and not just
in business. He was successful in life. He helped a
lot of people get started in business and encouraged
them to succeed. In fact, he bent over backwards to
help people. Actually, this perception took a little
time to form because my first impressions of him
came from his neighbors who despised him. When
my dad and I first started working at Charlie's farm,
the neighbors told me Charlie was in the Mafia, he

was running drugs from South America, and he ran a prostitution ring. They were jealous of his success and his money, and these stories were ways of venting their anger toward him.

But I didn't believe a word of it, especially after I got to know him and saw his heart for people. I saw a lot of things about the man that impressed me, and I wanted to be just like him. I grew up only two miles from Charlie's farm, and I'd always been impressed with his success, but as I interacted with him during those three months of contract work building levies, I liked what I saw in his character. I decided I wanted to pattern my life after his.

After I decided to work for Charlie, he gradually gave me more and more responsibility. The insurance business occupied a lot of his time, and in the early 90s, he didn't get to come to the farm as often as before. One day, though, he came to the farm. He was hauling rock in a dump truck, and he asked me to climb up into the truck because he wanted to talk to me. I climbed in and he told me he had given his life to Christ. That scared me. I didn't have much of a religious background at all. I had been to Vacation Bible School a couple of times when I was a kid, but that was probably at the end of a switch, so I wasn't too receptive to the message there! As an adult, I was turned off by Christians. In fact, I had told people, "Nobody better be thumping their Bible around me!" Now, here was the man I worked for and respected telling me he'd given his life to Christ. I went home and told my wife Betty what Charlie had said, then I announced to her, "I'm going to look for another place to work. I'm not going to put up with a bunch of this Bible thumping!" I thought Charlie had lost his mind . . . but maybe he was just going through a phase, and he'd grow out of it.

Still, I was curious about the things Charlie told me about the Lord. I asked Betty if we had a Bible, and she found one that she'd gotten many years before. It was covered with dust and had hardly ever been touched. I opened it and looked at some of the passages Charlie had talked about. I wanted to understand what Charlie had experienced.

At that time, my life was out of control. I was drinking a fifth of Scotch every couple of nights to get drunk and escape my problems. My relationship with Betty was empty. I worked hard on the farm, but my life was a disaster. During the days after Charlie told me he'd trusted Christ, I watched him very carefully. I thought Christians were people who prayed on Sunday and then shafted you on Monday, and I wanted to stay as far away from them as possible. But I saw a peace in Charlie's life I'd never seen before. He told me some things I'd never known or heard in my life. He explained that Jesus was God in human form, and by trusting in His death on the cross, I could be forgiven and have eternal life. (I don't know how a person could live his whole life in the middle of America and never hear those things, but it was all new to me.)

Only two weeks after Charlie first told me he'd trusted Christ, I climbed into that same dump truck with him and told him, "Charlie, I don't know what you've got, but I've got to have it, too." He led me through the prayer of salvation, and a huge burden lifted from my shoulders. I was so excited that I thought I'd save everybody in the adjoining counties by dark that day! Charlie laughed and said, "Jon, I may have to chain you down!" I was on fire for the Lord because I had found something everybody in this world needed.

I went home that night and told Betty, "I don't know how you're going to feel about this, but I trusted Christ today." She wept in happiness and hope. For days and months and years, I had sat in my chair every night getting drunk. Our marriage seemed beyond repair, and my anger was consuming me. My life lacked purpose and meaning. But now, things had changed. Through her tears, Betty said, "Jon, I want to trust Christ, too."

A couple of days later, I called Charlie and asked him to come over to our house. At our kitchen table, the three of us sat as Charlie explained the gospel to Betty. She was glad to hear that Good News, and she trusted the Lord on the spot. All of us cried because we were so happy.

God began to work a miracle in our hearts and in our relationship. God miraculously delivered me from alcohol. I stopped drinking Scotch immediately. I hadn't missed a day of drinking in 15 years, but I didn't have a single moment of withdrawal. It was a miracle. But I still drank a few beers in those first weeks. Then one day, I asked Charlie, "Is there any harm in drinking a few beers?"

He replied, "No, probably not, unless people are watching you and they become alcoholics because of your example." I sure didn't want that to happen, so I gave up beer that day. Chewing tobacco was a harder habit to kick. I tried to stop several times, but I failed each time. Finally, I asked a visiting preacher to pray for God's deliverance for me, and God gave me freedom from it that very moment.

Only thirteen months after Betty and I became Christians, she got sick. I took her to a doctor in Quincy, Illinois, and we learned that Betty had cancer. I called to tell Charlie, and he insisted that we take Betty to Kansas City to St. Luke's cancer wing. Charlie called his doctor and asked him to make time to see Betty. He confirmed the diagnosis, and the prognosis was not good.

Charlie, Betty, several others, and I prayed for 30 days for God to heal Betty. During that time, Betty underwent more cancer testing in Quincy, Illinois. The day Betty and I went to Quincy to get test results, God told her, "You're not sick. And you're not going to be sick." The doctors had scheduled her surgery, and they operated on her for seven hours. When they finished, the surgeon came over to me. He said, "Mr. Simmons, I want to see you privately."

I didn't think that was a good sign. I feared tragic news. But when we walked into an office, he told me, "Thirty days ago, your wife had an extensive case of cancer, but in the surgery today, I can't find any trace of it at all." God had healed her!

Charlie and I work incredibly well together. He's like a father to me, and we communicate very clearly and easily. As the vision for Heartland began to take shape in 1995, Charlie came to me and said, "Jon, we've got to figure out a way to make the farm a productive part of Heartland. I want to create jobs for people, but I don't want to lose money doing it." That made good sense to me. I prayed and God put the idea in my heart to change our operation from beef to a dairy. At the time, we had the second largest herd of black angus in the state, so it was going to be a big deal to change direction. When I told Charlie what God had said to me, he instantly confirmed the decision. He said, "Yes, that's what we need to do."

The dairy operation is very labor intensive, and it would provide lots of jobs for the people at Heartland. And it is a good business, too. My role with these young men in the Recovery Center is to provide jobs, but it is also to confront some of these men's hardened hearts from time to time. Confrontation isn't fun or easy, but it's sometimes necessary to get people on the right track. It is a part of my ministry and my contribution to these young men who are trusting God to turn their lives around. There are days I get a little tired of playing the heavy in their lives, but if I love them, I'll keep speaking the truth to them and encouraging them to learn and grow.

CHAPTER 9

LAURIE'S STORY

Author's note: You've read my account of my relationship with Laurie. Now I want you to get her side of the story. This chapter contains her story in her own words.

In February of 1981, I was working in Kansas City and living in an apartment with a roommate who was Charlie's secretary. My roommate fell in love with the company pilot, and they left to get married and then live in Kentucky. Before she left, she asked me if I was interested in her position in her company. It sounded exciting to me, so I decided to give it a try. Three interviews later, Charlie hired me to work for him.

My responsibilities consisted of knowing anything and everything associated with Charlie. Those first few weeks were beyond description! I tend to be quiet, shy, and withdrawn, and let me say, Charlie's not. I felt like I was hanging on with my fingernails to a speeding freight train! I was exhausted at the end of every single day, but I determined to hang on and see what happened.

Charlie's personality can be overwhelming. He's very bold, very aggressive. He's a visionary. These characteristics are the direct opposites of my personality. Sometimes after he walked out of the room I was left in my chair going, "Oh, why? Why am I here in this whirlwind?!"

When I came to Ozark, we had exactly one expandable file folder, unnamed, which referred to a "new company." This new company was eventually called National Insurance Services Corporation, which was the holding company for Charlie and the others to buy Ozark back from Bob Shaw. The summer of 1981, only a few months after I arrived, was when Charlie signed the contract with Bob Shaw to take the company back, supported by over 400 agents.

My role as Charlie's secretary meant we were constantly with each other. I went with him to regional sales meetings to take care of details for him. Before long, I was captivated by Charlie's charm and courage. I was only twenty-two years old, and he was, well, older! Both of us worked long after others left the office at five o'clock each day, and going to dinner together was merely a convenience. I enjoyed being with him, and I guess he enjoyed being with me. Soon, however, Charlie asked me to dinner even when it wasn't just for convenience. That was a big step forward in our relationship.

My parents found out I was spending time with Charlie, and they were less than enthusiastic about our relationship. They weren't the only ones; I had plenty of doubts about it myself. He was six months older than my father, and I was "dating" him! I wasn't dating anybody my own age, so in effect, I was eliminating any other possibilities for the future. And our personalities are so different. He's bold. He's always on the run, and he doesn't sit down. I'm not like that. I asked myself a thousand times, *Is this the life I want? Is this what I want to do? Is this the man I want to be with the rest of my life . . . or do I want someone with a nice, white picket fence and little children?*

Charlie is much more romantic than I am. He took me to fine restaurants for candlelight dinners, wine, and flowers. No one could have been sweeter or more generous to me than Charlie was. And I loved him. For several years, our relationship went up and down. Sometimes I answered my questions about the relationship "yes," and sometimes I answered them "no." Charlie was having the same questions, but from the other side: *Do I want to lock this young girl into a relationship with an old guy like me? Is it fair to her?*

I enjoyed the work I was doing for Charlie and the company. There was never a dull moment! The agents were doing a fantastic job, and the company was growing. Charlie was the first agent, and so his heart had a real passion for the others. Leroy Ellsworth had been in charge of the agency department to help the agents with licensing, provide them with information, and assist them with anything else they needed to do their jobs. Leroy left the company in 1985. We had not replaced him, so that department essentially ran itself. After two years of neglect, it was not operating efficiently or effectively. A lot of mistakes were being made in regard to the state and federal insurance regulations, so in 1987, Charlie asked me if I would oversee the agency department.

Taking over that department was a little overwhelming. I knew bits and pieces of what was demanded in that job just by being Charlie's secretary, but two years of inattention in the agency department had taken their toll. The job had become a huge task. I dived in and tried to make heads or tails of all the details and loose ends that had piled up. The job was daunting, but it felt good to be trusted with such an important responsibility at Ozark.

For five years, Charlie and I lived on a rollercoaster of love and doubt. When I was twenty-seven, I felt like I needed to get off that ride and make a decision—one way or the other. I thought about it long and hard (as if I hadn't for the past five years!), and after a lot of soul-searching, I came to a firm conclusion. I told Charlie, "We need to stop seeing each other."

As soon as I told him, I felt lost and alone. I desperately wanted to be with him, and after a few traumatic days and long, sleepless nights, I told him I had changed my mind. I thought that had settled the matter forever, but in the months that followed, we continued to ride that dreaded rollercoaster. Sometimes we separated for months, intending to break off our relationship. After all, no matter what we were feeling, Charlie is thirty-one years older than I am. I wondered, *Is this the right thing to do? Is it right to have a relationship with a man thirty-one years older? What is life going to be like, then, for me when he passes on? The basic odds are that he will die before I do.* Age difference . . . personality differences . . . we had plenty of reasons to doubt. Still. . . .

The relationship seemed doomed from the beginning (as my parents had told me), but something kept pulling us together. Charlie and I were polar opposites in so many ways, but we respected each other, and we felt genuine affection for each other. Those things encouraged us time and again to pursue our relationship and try to make it work—in spite of everything.

Finally, in September of 1989, after one last pang of doubt, Charlie decided to ask me to marry him. After dinner one night, he gave me a ring and said, "If you think this is the right thing to do, let's get married."

I said, "Yes," and it was settled. Finally!

My parents and my friends who had expressed their concern early in our relationship didn't object. I was worried, however, about the response of Charlie's brother Wilbur and his wife. They were strong Christians, and I was afraid they would try to talk Charlie out of marrying a "kid" like me. When Charlie called to

> Charlie and I were polar opposites in so many ways, but we respected each other, and we felt genuine affection for each other.

tell them, I was ready for the bombs to drop. To my surprise, they were very excited and supportive!

We kept our engagement a secret except for family and a few close friends. We wanted to surprise everybody else, so we planned to get married in Bermuda at our annual convention after Christmas. We brought invitations and slipped them under the doors on the afternoon of December 30. That evening, our annual insurance convention turned into a wedding!

I wore a blue wedding dress. (Blue is Charlie's favorite color.) When we walked in, many of the agents were shocked. They had to see it to believe it. Charlie had been divorced for twenty-five years, and though we had dated for a long time, many of them didn't think he would ever get married.

I was thirty-one years old and very independent. If a person has been single and working until that age, she gets fairly set into a routine. I worked hard at Ozark, and I was proud of how I accomplished my job. In many ways, that responsibility defined who I was. I suppose because I enjoyed my word so much, it became my identity. I had my own way of working, my own way of relaxing, and my own way of handling stress. Now, suddenly, I was living with the most dynamic, powerful man I had ever known. And he expected things to be done his way.

The tension points flared up all day every day, from the sublime to the ridiculous, from the petty to the monumental. Most of them occurred when we simply didn't consider the feelings and wants of each other. Without even

talking to me, Charlie sometimes made decisions that affected us both. When I complained, he was surprised. But I did the same thing. In my independence, I made choices without considering Charlie at all, and of course, he didn't appreciate it. These offenses multiplied, and the tension mounted. We talked to try to resolve things, but that only seemed to make the situation worse. The rollercoaster we had been on for so many years now stayed stuck at the bottom. The only breaks in the tension occurred when Charlie traveled. When he walked out the door, I felt independent again. For a few days I could relax . . . but then Charlie came back and the tension returned.

After about a year and a half of marriage, I began to have anxiety attacks. They came when he would leave town. This really confused me. I didn't care that he left town. In fact, I was glad for him to leave. *So,* I thought, *Why is this bothering me that he' s not her e?*

The anxiety attacks became all-consuming: heart palpitations, fear, shortness of breath. The fear was most disturbing. I had no idea why I was so afraid, especially when Charlie left town and I could be independent again.

I thought I was losing my mind. I tried to will the attacks away, but that didn't work. At the same time, my head was splitting with the pain of migraine headaches. My doctor prescribed various drugs, and I thought the panic attacks might be a reaction to the drugs.

> The anxiety attacks became all-consuming: heart palpitations, fear, shortness of breath. The fear was most disturbing.

I went from one doctor to another to find relief. Each one tried a different prescription medicine, but none helped. My hope was fading away. Finally, a doctor looked at my records of so many different prescriptions given by so many different physicians, and he took me off all the medications for the migraines. My head still hurt, and I still experienced the panic attacks. As a last resort, I wondered if maybe God could help. I was desperate to find some answers, so I decided to go back to church with my parents. They are Catholics, so I went to mass with them at their church in Overland Park. I'm not sure what I expected to get by going to church with them, but I was clinging to any shred of hope. I needed help anywhere I could find it.

I went to church for several weeks, but the panic attacks continued to grow worse. I had thoroughly enjoyed my work at Ozark for many years, yet even the simplest tasks had become a challenge. I could no longer do my job well! My identity was shattered. I needed help!

During my discussions with Charlie over the years, he had occasionally referred to his belief in God and his experience with organized religion, though it certainly wasn't a subject that came up often. There were no in-depth discussions of faith or Christ, and we certainly didn't go to church. After I started going back to church with my parents, I decided to tell Charlie what I was doing. He had been out of town, and I was praying when he returned. I thought, *This is the time to tell him.*

Charlie walked in carrying his hanging bag of clothes. My Catholic prayer book was open in my hands. I had no idea how he would respond, so I was working up my courage to explain to him that I was going to church. But before I could say a word, Charlie saw the prayer book and said, "What are you doing?"

"I'm praying!"

He walked past me into the bedroom to put up his bag, then he came back in. He announced, "Do you want to know what's the matter with you? The Lord's dealing with your heart."

That was a really strange thing for him to say. As little as he talked about God, I had no clue what he was talking about. I asked him, "God's dealing with my heart? What does that mean?"

Charlie then explained the plan of salvation to me and told me how I could be saved. It was so strange to hear Charlie explain Christ's plan of salvation when I had never heard him say anything like this in nine years together. But I was desperate at that point, so I'd listen to anything.

Charlie told me I needed to ask Christ into my heart. He told me to repent. He said I needed to go to the Lord and acknowledge I was sinner and wanted to be forgiven. I had grown up a Catholic, so the idea of salvation by faith in Christ seemed new to me. I was familiar with confessing sins, and I certainly was willing to confess anything to stop the pain in my life. I got alone and prayed, "God, I don't want to live this way. I was wondering if you can get me out of this jam. I'm miserable here."

Nothing happened, so I did it again. And again and again and again. Now I was *really* confused. After all these futile attempts, I told Charlie, "This isn't working."

Charlie said, "You're not desperate enough."

I thought, *Oh boy , if I'm not desperate enough, who is!? I don' t know what "desperate" could possibly mean if it doesn'   t describe me!*

On November 25, 1992, I was getting ready to go to work. In our dressing room, I was putting on my makeup. I decided to pray again, so I got down on my knees and I said, "Lord, I don't know what desperate is, but I'm desperate! If this is all life is, I don't want to do this anymore. You've got to do something."

> I thought, *Oh boy, if I'm not desperate enough, who is!? I don't know what "desperate" could possibly mean if it doesn't describe me!*

And God flooded me with His peace! He spoke to my heart and said, "I am here! It's okay." He made Himself real to me, and the burden of the anxiety lifted. I no longer felt like fear was overpowering and consuming me. I was so relieved! For the first time, I had a great sense of joy in my heart. It was great!

I finished dressing and rushed to the office. I was so excited to tell Charlie! I went into his office and blurted out, "I've got the Lord!" Charlie was so happy tears started running down his cheeks.

We savored the moment. I said again, "I met the Lord. It's done. I met the Lord." And Charlie just cried. As I walked out, I thought, *This is r eally strange. Charlie' s crying, and I feel good for a change.*

On Sunday a few days later, Charlie got me up and said, "Let's go to church." His nephew was a pastor at New Life Community Church who had invited us to attend many times, and this time we went. After the sermon, Charlie's nephew asked people who wanted to respond to the Lord's invitation to come to the altar. Charlie nudged my elbow and went forward. I knew that he was rededicating his life to the Lord. Later, Charlie told me he had known for days that he was going to recommit his life to Christ that morning, but he hadn't said a word to me about it before the altar call.

The pastor told me to buy a study Bible to help me understand God's truth better. I bought one immediately, and for the next few days, my nose never came out of it. It was suddenly like a terrific, page-turning novel. The pastor told me to highlight passages that touched my heart, so I started underlining passage after passage. The whole spiritual world opened up to me as I read the Bible! He told me to start in the book of John, and to read it through. Then I went back and started over. The study helps and the center column notes helped a lot. In less than three months, I read through the New Testament.

During these weeks I saw Charlie's relationship with God become strong again. I was starting out new and fresh, so it was a little different for me than for him. Charlie said that when he rededicated his life, the Lord picked up just where he left off. Charlie experienced such cleansing that it seemed all those years in between his spiritual life vanished. He felt the joy and the power of the Lord again, which was good because I needed the stability of somebody who was more mature in the faith than I was. I needed someone to give me insight and to correct me when I was off base. Sometimes when Charlie and I talked about a passage, he told me, "Whoa! Boy, were you wrong on that one! Here's what it means. . . ." I watched Charlie flourish and blossom in God's love. That was totally unique and different.

Part of what God was doing in Charlie's life was softening him. Charlie was a bold, aggressive, visionary who never had a doubt about himself or his direction. But when he rededicated his life, he became more circumspect, less aggressive and domineering. This new attitude continued until the time God called him to pastor the church of Heartland in 1995. When God told Charlie to build a church there, Charlie assumed somebody else would be the pastor. For several months, we knew God wanted us to start the church. The only question was: who was going to pastor? We kept praying for a pastor, and finally, God showed us Charlie was His man for the job. To be honest, Charlie was a little nervous. Of course, he never said he was nervous, but I could tell he felt the weight of responsibility to lead well . . . and not mess up like he did last time.

> I watched Charlie flourish and blossom in God's love. That was totally unique and different.

As Charlie prayed and as he studied, I could see growth in him. I could see the changes that were occurring in his life. He was growing in his faith, and he was blossoming. At one point, God gave Charlie a vision of young people raising their hands praising God at Heartland. Charlie knew it was from God, and he knew he needed to respond. He began planning and building all the facilities there, but my heart wasn't in it. I was glad for Charlie, but I felt comfortable in my new faith and in my old job at Ozark. That was enough change for me at the time.

In an evening service at New Life Community Church, God illuminated for me that the vision for Heartland was not just "a Charlie thing." That night, for the first time, God showed me that He was at work at Heartland. It is His ministry, His vision, and He is accomplishing His purposes there. This experience was so real to me that I thought, *Uh, oh. We're going to have to move.* But moving from Kansas City to Shelby County was not on my agenda. I was established at Ozark, and I had planned to stay there and work in the agency department for the rest of my life.

But that night I realized my plans were going to change. Charlie had been the visionary, and Heartland had been his vision. We had operated somewhat separately all through our marriage. Charlie was very interested in the farm and the cattle business, and now he had a ministry that involved those things. That was fine . . . as long as I could stay in Kansas City and visit the farm for short periods of time. But now, all that was changing. The stability of my work—and my identity—was going to be shaken.

I didn't tell Charlie that I knew God said Heartland was "a God thing" and not "a Charlie thing," and that we would be moving to the farm. For several months, I kept this between God and me. Finally, I told Charlie it was time for me to join him in the Heartland ministry heart, soul, and body. He was thrilled! Shocked . . . but thrilled. Charlie started crying. He had wanted me to be excited about Heartland, but he didn't want to force it on me. He had told God, "You are going to have to deal with Laurie. If You want her at Heartland, You'll have to give her the desire to go." Charlie knew that if he tried to make it happen, I would think it was just more of his aggressive, make-it-happen ways, so he backed off completely. In fact, he didn't even mention the idea to me. That says a lot about the change God was working in his heart. At about this time, we started Heartland Community Church.

We also began to look for someone to replace me in the agency department at Ozark. For some reason, the people we interviewed didn't work out. I had been at Ozark a long time, and there were a lot of intangibles I knew that a new person wouldn't understand. Our department was responsible to take care of the 900 insurance agents who represented Ozark across the country. We helped them with their licensing and their compensation. It was our job to provide them with whatever they needed to be successful. Al Weber was the new Executive Vice President. He had been here only a short while, and he wasn't comfortable with my leaving a void in the agency department. For that reason, we began a slow weaning process that lasted almost three years. By 1998 the transition was complete, so I moved permanently from Kansas City to Heartland. There would be no more three days here and four days there. Now my body—and my heart—were at Heartland.

I tease Charlie all the time about his soft heart. He wants to help everybody in need, but of course, that's not possible. Still, he tries to help as many people as he can. When he began Heartland, Charlie listened carefully to the needs of parents and children. I began to listen, too. About a month before we moved to the farm, a teenage girl, Holly, and her mother visited Heartland. I wasn't at the farm, so I didn't meet them. They returned shortly after we moved, and they stayed in our home. I heard their story and I felt a lot of compassion for them. My brother had been an addict for twenty-four years. I know the pain of the parents and how one person's addiction consumes the whole family. My heart went out to them. I hated to see the mother's desperation. She told me, "I've got to do something with this child!" The relationship between Holly and her mother had deteriorated. Trust had evaporated, and they had almost no communication. They needed help, and they needed it now! But we didn't have any openings in our houses for another teenager. I told Charlie, "We'd better step in and help Holly."

> My heart went out to them. I hated to see the mother's desperation.

Certain aspects of Charlie's and my life together are hard for young people to comprehend. We fly in a private jet to and from Kansas City. They see the thousands of acres we own. They meet senators and congressmen who come to visit Heartland. They overhear Charlie making hundred-thousand-dollar decisions about crops, cows, and equipment on a daily basis. Such behavior can be very deceptive to a young person who may think everybody deserves to live this way. Someone with a life-controlling problem doesn't need any additional deceptive fantasies of wealth and the easy life to add to their existing problems. For that reason, I was hesitant to have anyone live with us. But the only other option was to turn this young woman away without giving her the help she needed. I wasn't willing to do that.

Since then, Charlie and I have invited several young women to live in our home. We are now house parents just like the others at Heartland. We try very hard to make sure our responsibilities at Ozark and Charlie's management of this land, dairy, school, and ministry don't distort these young people's expectations. We are two people who are submitting to the lordship of Jesus Christ every minute of every day. I trust that this commitment overshadows the awkwardness of running large businesses and shaping the ministry at Heartland.

Holly was in our home only a few days when the games began, and I don't mean Monopoly or Twister. I'm talking about trying to control other people through whining, anger, self-pity, and withdrawal. These games are played in virtually every home where addictions and other life-controlling problems exist, but Charlie and I were determined not to play them in our home. That's a difficult assignment because many people are exceptionally good at them!

Holly had a rotten attitude for the first thirty days. She was cold and unresponsive to our love for her. She refused to participate in any activity, and she rebelled against our authority at every turn. She became very moody. These were the techniques she had used to upset her mother and control her home life. From my background, I could spot it a mile away! And I had a solution: the moodier she got, the happier I got. I wasn't angry with her. I understood her goals and methods. She was doing the things that had worked with her mom . . . but they weren't going to work with me.

I threw her off balance by not reacting to her moods. When she was happy, I was happy. And when she pouted, I remained happy. That confused her a lot! In addition, we let Holly know we are praying people, and we were going to ask God to work in her life, reveal her sin, and give her the power to repent. Over time, we repeated to her over and over again: God was going to work in her life to show her that game-playing is destructive to her and to those around her.

> I threw her off balance by not reacting to her moods. When she was happy, I was happy. And when she pouted, I remained happy. That confused her a lot!

Like Holly, other teenagers who come to live with us try to play games. Some of them are pregnant; some are on drugs; some have run away from home several times; and many of them have a combination of these problems. They come with different stories and with different goals, but we have just one goal for every person who walks in our door: that they would fall in love with Jesus Christ and serve Him the rest of their lives.

When they first come, many young women have a counterproductive short-term goal: to avoid responsibility for their behavior. Their solution to life's stress is to drink or use drugs to deaden the pain. Their answer to their longing for love is to have sex. Their method of resolving conflict is to run from it. These methods seem to work for a while, but eventually cause even *more* stress, longing, and conflict. As we provide a loving, stable environment and refuse to play their games, our young women are forced to confront the reality of their deepest needs. At that teachable moment, they can cry out to God, the one who can mend their broken hearts and give them the strength to change those destructive patterns of behavior.

Rachel and Tommy

About two years ago, two children were brought to Heartland: five-year-old Rachel and her brother, Tommy, who was four. The Missouri Department of Family Services had taken them from their parents once before and had brought them to Heartland for foster care. The parents, who were guilty of abuse and neglect, promised to change, so DFS let the children return to them. But after only three or four months, DFS brought these children back to us in the middle of the night. People in the community had seen the parents with a third child, a baby named Betty, who had suddenly vanished without a trace. In addition, the two older children bore new scars of abuse. Strangely, there were no records of any kind about Betty: no birth certificate, no medical records, no Social Security number. Nothing. She had simply vanished.

Rachel wore her hair very long. When anyone approached her, she squatted down on the floor and put her head down so her hair covered her face. That was her way of hiding from any interaction with an adult.

Tommy had a different defense. If anyone got near him, he would spit, bite, kick, and hit. The Birches were Tommy's and Rachel's house parents. When they tried to put Tommy in a car seat, they ended up bruised from their efforts. This little boy was very much like an animal.

Rachel was almost totally unresponsive to human contact. She couldn't carry on a conversation. If someone wanted her to do something, she had to be given very specific instructions. Then she responded like a robot.

Initially, neither of the children talked about their home life. But after a while, Tommy approached the Birches and announced, "I don't want you to call me Tommy anymore."

She asked, "Why?"

"That's my dad's name," Tommy answered. "And I don't want to be called by my dad's name." Tommy's middle name was John, so Mrs. Birch suggested, "Do you want to be called 'Jack'?" He smiled, "Yes, you can call me Jack." In fact, he went to everyone in the community and at church and told them, "Call me Jack."

This was a significant turning point. Once this little boy separated himself from the name "Tommy," he had the ability to detach.

One day Mrs. Birch watched as Rachel read a magazine, *Homes and Gardens*. The little girl looked intently at a photograph of a garden, then she looked up and said, "That looks like where Betty is."

Mrs. Birch quickly came to Charlie and me and told us about Rachel's remark. We contacted DFS, and they launched an immediate investigation. They looked in every garden to search for possible grave sites, and they talked to every person in the community. They learned that Betty had been seen just before Halloween, but she hadn't been seen since.

Jack was then questioned by DFS, and he sang like a little songbird! He answered all their questions and painted a vivid picture of what had happened in that home. Jack was being trained as a Satanist. The boys were taught to beat girls and abuse them sexually. Among other things, Jack had beaten his sister viciously with a belt. Out of her rage, Rachel took every opportunity to take revenge and hurt her brother.

After the DFS officials got this information from Jack, they filed charges of criminal child abuse against both parents. In court, the judge told them they had a choice of giving up their parental rights to Rachel and Jack, or the police would file charges for the murder of their baby, Betty. To save their own hides, they signed the papers on the spot. The state put the two children up for adoption, and both of them were adopted by families at Heartland.

Of course, our entire Heartland community supported these children. As we became aware of the demonic dimension of the abuse these children had suffered, we wanted to take definitive action. As the pastor, Charlie took the initiative to gather some men to pray to bind the power of Satan in these young lives and reclaim them for Jesus Christ. In Sunday School one morning, Charlie and Ervin Rutherford went to Rachel's class. Because of her background and the fact that adults who touched her had often hurt or abused her, they wanted to be careful to avoid scaring her. Charlie's great-granddaughter, Courtney, was in Rachel's class, so they smiled, walked over to Courtney, and laid hands on her while they prayed for her. One by one, they did the same for each child in the class. The last one in the circle was Rachel. They prayed that God would bless this little girl in a deep, special way, that the love of Jesus would shatter the darkness in her life, and she would feel the Spirit of God in her heart. When they finished praying, little Rachel beamed!

Shortly after that, in a worship service on a Sunday night, one of the teenage girls who lived in the Birches' home brought Rachel to the altar. Again, Charlie had the opportunity to lay hands on this precious girl and pray for her.

A few weeks later, Charlie and I were in Kansas City when we got a phone call that Rachel had accepted the Lord that day. We returned to Heartland for the Wednesday night service at the church. Rachel was waiting at the door because she wanted to tell Pastor Charlie herself that she had accepted Jesus. That was a real turning point for her. Her tendencies to lash out and hurt her brother stopped. Almost immediately, this uptight, withdrawn, "robot" child became warm, responsive, and affectionate. It was a true miracle of God's great grace!

One day in Rachel's kindergarten class, a number of the kids were out sick. During Bible study time, the teacher told the children, "I sense the presence of God! Do you?" They nodded, and she asked them, "Would you like me to pray for you to receive a special blessing of God's love?"

"Sure!" "OK!" "Yeah!"

This dear teacher prayed with these kids and every single one of them felt God's wonderful love and power in a special, new way. They didn't want to keep this blessing to themselves. These little kindergartners went through the rest of the school laying hands on the other kids and praying for them. It was incredible!

During the altar call the next Sunday, Rachel came up next to Charlie and, like him, laid hands on people and prayed for them. And like Charlie, this little girl had tears of compassion for the lost and hurting. As I watched, I thought of that little girl months before who had fallen to the floor in a ball and hidden her face in her hair to avoid any meaningful contact with people. Now she was ministering the love of God out of a full heart of God's grace and mercy.

"Out of the mouths of babes. . . ," the Bible says, but in this case, it was "out of the hearts of babes." God can do amazing things through people who love Him—even little people.

This is what Heartland is all about. Nothing more. Nothing less.

CHAPTER 10

LOOKING BACK . . .

LOOKING FORWARD

I don't view anything I do for people as sacrifice. I help people as much as I can because it's only right. Putting others ahead of ourselves is not above and beyond the call of duty. I give my father great credit for all the good things that have happened in my life. I followed many of his principles, but I didn't keep them all. And if I had stuck to them more closely, many of the hard times I've experienced would never have happened.

My Dad trusted people, but he wasn't naive. He was very astute. He had only a third-grade education, but he was brilliant. He was honest to a fault, and he was straightforward in all his dealings with people. If he thought he had taken unfair advantage of someone, he went back to straighten things out. Not many people would do that! Dad was careful with his money, but he was very generous. He didn't like to have anybody else pay for a meal, so he made sure he got to the cash register first. What money he had, he managed carefully. I learned a lot from my father. He was an incredible example of caring for people who can never repay acts of kindness. Though for years he didn't know the Lord, he still exemplified the goodness of God on a daily basis.

When you are willing to set aside your own agenda and simply walk with the Lord, it is amazing what God will do. He leads, He brings in people to help, and He gives peace even in the middle of problems. God has orchestrated the past for His present purposes. Many of us look at the past and think, *Man, I messed up big time!* or *What a tragedy! My life will never be the same.* We wish the past was different. We need to realize that God was sovereignly at work in the past to weave circumstances and relationships to accomplish His will. And the situations we find ourselves in today—situations that seem to be a million miles away from the heart and hand of God—are somehow a part of the tapestry God is weaving to accomplish His gracious will. That gives us hope and peace.

> And the situations we find ourselves in today—situations that seem to be a million miles away from the heart and hand of God—are somehow a part of the tapestry God is weaving to accomplish His gracious will. That gives us hope and peace.

One of the most encouraging stories in the Bible is the saga of Joseph, the eleventh (and favorite) son of Jacob. As a young man, Joseph had two dreams one night. He told his family that in both dreams, they all bowed before him—even his parents! His brothers were outraged, and they plotted to get rid of "this dreamer."

Jacob sent Joseph to check up on his brothers as they tended the family flocks. As he approached, the brothers schemed to kill him and throw him into a pit. They would cover the murder by telling their father a wild animal had killed him. Reuben, the oldest brother, convinced his brothers to throw Joseph into a cistern instead, keeping him alive. Reuben planned to sneak back and rescue Joseph.

With Joseph in the pit and Reuben away for a while the other brothers saw a passing caravan and sold Joseph to the traders. They had gotten rid of Joseph and made some money in the bargain! To cover their crime, they dipped Joseph's coat—a treasured gift from his father—in goat's blood to simulate a wild animal attack. Then they took the coat back to Jacob, who wept bitterly over the loss of his son.

Meanwhile the caravan arrived in Egypt, and Joseph was sold to an official named Potiphar. Joseph proved to be a capable administrator, and Potiphar flourished. Potiphar's wife, however, had designs on young, handsome Joseph. She tried to seduce him, but he refused. As he ran from her, she grabbed his cloak. She showed it to Potiphar and told her husband Joseph had tried to rape her. As a result, Joseph was thrown into prison. He had been a good son, but was betrayed by his brothers. Now he had been a good servant and was betrayed by his master's wife, landing in the recesses of an Egyptian dungeon. Had God abandoned him? Did Joseph complain of how unfair God was? No. His faith held strong.

After years in that dungeon, Joseph's cell became crowded with two of the pharaoh's servants, a baker and a cupbearer. Each of these men had a dream, and Joseph interpreted them. The cupbearer heard good news: he would be restored to his position. But the baker learned his dream was a death sentence: he would be executed. Joseph's interpretations proved true. As the jailer led the exultant cupbearer to freedom, Joseph asked him to remember him.

But the freed cupbearer promptly forgot about Joseph, so Joseph continued to languish in the prison. Still, Joseph's faith was strong; he refused to complain. Some time later, the pharaoh had a dream. None of his wise men could interpret it for him. He became desperate to know what it meant! The cupbearer finally remembered Joseph, and he told the pharaoh about Joseph's ability to interpret dreams. The pharaoh immediately sent for Joseph, who stood before the most powerful man in the world and told him what his dream meant. The pharaoh rewarded Joseph by making him prime minister, the second in command over all Egypt!

Pharaoh's dreams had foretold years of plenty to be followed by years of famine, so Joseph stored grain during the good years to provide in the lean ones. In those years of famine, the family of Jacob needed food, so Jacob sent ten of his sons to Egypt. When they arrived, they bowed before the prime minister. (Do you remember Joseph's dreams?) Joseph didn't reveal himself right away. Through a series of events, the betrayed brother tested those who had sold him into slavery to see if their hearts had changed. Finally, they proved they were now faithful and honorable, so Joseph finally said, "I am Joseph, your brother."

They were shocked—and very much afraid! They had every reason to believe Joseph would extract vengeance on them and punish them for what they had done to him years before.

But Joseph had a completely different outlook, one he had gained in his youth and which had been sharpened in years of slavery and captivity: God's purposes are higher and better than man's.

His brothers then came and threw themselves down before him. "We are your slaves," they said. But Joseph said to them, "Don't be afraid. Am I in the place of God? You intended it to harm me, but God intended it for good to accomplish what is now being done, the saving of many lives" (Genesis 50:18-20).

Even though his brothers' actions were motivated by evil and carried out in malice, Joseph knew God could bring good out of what had been done. Never in all those years do we hear Joseph express the whines of self-pity. Never in all those years do we see him shake his fist at God for all the injustice. No, we only see him believe that a good and sovereign God reigns in the earth. Joseph knew God can be trusted even when men cannot be.

We experience difficulties because of our own sins and the sins of others. We may be victims of a personal, willful attack, or we may experience the unintended backwash of the consequences of another's mistakes. No matter what the circumstance, God is bigger. No matter what the motivation, God is sovereign and will weave it into His purposes. If Joseph could cling to the goodness and the will of God amid his incredible difficulties, you and I can surely do the same.

Mistakes don't ruin our lives. Instead, it is how we handle our mistakes that either builds or destroys our lives. If we blame ourselves or others for dumb choices or hurtful actions, we will only dig a deeper pit. A far more positive response is to say, "Lord, what do You want me to learn from this? I'm listening, Lord."

I have experienced betrayal by some of my best friends, heartaches I have inflicted on myself, and a host of other problems caused by a wide array of sources. But through all these trials I knew I couldn't waste my time feeling sorry for myself or being bitter at others. God was saying, "Hey, Charlie, pay attention! Quit fooling around and get your act together. I'm going to keep these things coming your way until you get the message." God guided me with warnings and corrections even when I wasn't walking with Him. That's how great His love is! Sometimes I paid attention, and sometimes I didn't. I never openly defied God, but sometimes I acted like I didn't hear him.

No matter what the circumstance, God is bigger.

I hurt many people by my sinfulness. After Wanda and I divorced, I was married to my business but I was a still a young, single, and lonely man. Before long, I began to engage in sexual sin. I tried to develop real relationships with each of a series of women, but I was genuinely addicted to sex.

Sexual sin drove a wedge between me and God. I knew it was wrong; I had preached on the subject many times. But for some reason, it became an obsession in my life. I was able to keep my business life and my personal life separate. People in the company knew I was sinning in this way, but they also knew I never let it interfere with business. I never missed a meeting or an appointment because I was on a date. I never lost focus at work because I was preoccupied with thinking about a woman. The women in the company felt completely safe, and their husbands knew they had nothing to fear from me. I never had relations with any married women or any agents in the company. I made sure people in the business were never hurt by my behavior.

Sometimes people who come to the Recovery Center at Heartland ask sincerely, "Charlie, I'm an alcoholic. What do you know about addictions?" I can tell them I know very well what an addiction is and how it consumes and deceives a person. I know because I experienced an addiction myself. And I also know very well what it means for Jesus Christ to deliver someone from an addiction because I was delivered from mine. It is a mark of the incredible mercy of God that He didn't give up on me all those years. He kept calling me back to Him. Because God finally delivered me from that evil, I believe He can help anyone with any addiction.

My deliverance didn't come easily. First, I had to admit I had a problem. That may sound very obvious, but addicts have incredible difficulty admitting their problem. They excuse it; they say it's normal; they say it doesn't hurt anybody; and they go to great lengths to deny the problem even exists. Addiction may have some qualities of a disease. Doctors and psychologists have debated that for years, but one thing I know: it is sin. And sins demand repentance. When we put something or someone in the place of God in our lives in an effort to find counterfeit peace, direction, and fulfillment, we need to repent. When we put a substance, a behavior, or a person in the center of our lives and allow it to control us, that is idolatry. We need to confess that sin and trust in a merciful, powerful God to change our hearts and our behavior. One of the motivations to change is to realize that our sin destroys lives: our own and others. Until we are convinced of that, we will tolerate the problem. But when we come to grips with the pain and heartache sin causes, and see how it separates us from the One who loves us so much, we can find the drive and the courage to repent.

> **But when we come to grips with the pain and heartache sin causes, and see how it separates us from the One who loves us so much, we can find the drive and the courage to repent.**

Many people swap addictions, dealing with one problem by delving into another one. They go from drugs to sex, or sex to meetings, or food to cigarettes, or cigarettes to something else. Only Jesus

Christ can fill the huge hole in our souls so the craving goes away. This is a spiritual, miraculous work of God. Deliverance can happen in an instant, and only then will the task of retraining our habits be successful. If we try to only change habits without the supernatural work of God in our hearts, we will fail. I've seen it far too often to doubt it. Repentance involves both the immediate and the continual: an immediate decision to change and trust God, and the day to day task of choosing to think healthy, positive thoughts and making decisions to act righteously. God provides strength for both.

Even after I was saved, I struggled with my sexual urges. I was faithful to Laurie all the time we were married, but it was incredibly hard. And in those first years of our marriage, the problems in our marriage made it even more difficult to stay faithful. I made a rock-solid commitment to live faithfully with Laurie, and even after we were saved, we had to rely on that commitment because sometimes our feelings of love simply were not strong.

In all those years of being alone, I had become an island. No matter what happened, I was determined to be strong and kind. Nobody was going to see me sweat! That served me well as a company president, but it didn't serve me well as a husband. Even when I went through personal bankruptcy, going in a single day from assets of five million dollars to a debt of over three million dollars, my personality didn't change much at all. I remained as upbeat and positive as I had always been. Nobody knew I no longer owned a car. Nobody knew my furniture had been confiscated. I came to the office every day and acted like everything was fine. I think people appreciated the sense of security I communicated, but the negative side of that strength was that I didn't know how to let Laurie inside the walls of my heart. As my wife, she expected me to open up to her. When I couldn't unlock those parts of my heart as I kept up the strong facade, she recoiled. When she withdrew, I backed away even farther. It was a terrible dance, and we moved in those steps day after day.

In fact, the hardest period of our marriage came after both of us were saved. It was a matter of survival day to day, or our marriage was going to crumble. We had to depend on God every day to help us work things out. It was a very, very hard time for both of us, and if it hadn't been for God, we would never have made it.

In our country, half of first marriages fail, and sixty-five percent of second marriages end in divorce. The odds were against us, but God was on our side. The very things that built our relationship when we dated threatened to destroy us after we were married. She had admired my strength, but then she despised me for dominating her. In many ways, she was right. I had lived by myself for twenty-five years doing what I wanted to do. Suddenly, I was married, but I still made all my own decisions. Laurie expected me (very rightly, I might add) to ask her opinion and consult her about decisions that affected both of us, but that never crossed my mind—until the lid blew off from time to time! Before we married, she seemed to enjoy and appreciate my ability to make decisions, but after we said,

"I do," those same qualities seemed to make her far too dependent on me. On the other hand, I had loved her gentleness when we dated, but after we married I perceived it as weakness.

Instead of resolving these conflicts, they drove us farther and farther apart until we didn't even like each other. I wish I could say everything instantly changed when we trusted Christ, but it didn't. The devil kept using the churning, unforgotten (and unforgiven) mass of past hurts to fan the flames of the twin evils: disdain and apathy. Many days neither of us thought we could go on, but we determined—every minute of every day—to cling to the Lord and trust Him to change us. Satan tried to destroy us. If he destroyed our marriage, the ministry at Heartland would have been destroyed, too.

God, however, was at work preparing Laurie and me and the business for an outpouring of His Spirit at Heartland, but He had to accomplish one major step before the blessing would come: making complete peace between Laurie and me. Both of us determined to stop resenting the other's weaknesses and faults and to love each other no matter what. Love is not just a feeling; it is a rock-solid commitment to move beyond your feelings, treasure the other person, and do what is best for that person. I realized that if I couldn't love Laurie with all my heart, I couldn't love

> Love is not just a feeling; it is a rock-solid commitment to move beyond your feelings, treasure the other person, and do what is best for that person.

Christ either. There was no instantaneous breakthrough that suddenly solved all our problems, but there was a day of decision to love one another no matter what the cost. Since that decision, our relationship has grown day by day. I look back now and see incredible change in both of us. The change in our relationship was so gradual that we couldn't detect it from one day to the next, but like an oak tree that grows strong over time, we grew as a couple—straight and tall in the soil of God's love and the rain of daily choices to care for each other.

It is very sobering to realize I had a wonderful relationship with God many years ago—and lost it. I can't point to any event or any single decision that ruined what I had. As I think back on those years of sin, I am astounded that I turned away from the Lord. I never said, "I'm an evil person, and I don't want God." Even during my years of sin, I told people who were in trouble, "Look, God is God, and He can be your Savior."

One result of turning back to God a few years ago is that now I am even more convinced of the incredible love of God, just as the Prodigal Son came to realize his father's forgiveness and love in a richer way than his brother. That doesn't justify the sin, but through repentance we can experience God's wonderful cleansing and compassion. I am so convinced of His love that I long to be with Him. That's why I have such convictions about prayer. In the same way, the reason people don't pray and the reason people don't love God is because they believe God is harsh or that He simply doesn't care about them. If someone believes either of those things, he or she won't pray (except maybe out a sense of duty and guilt). The majority of people do not believe God is interested in their day-to-day activities. They think God started the world in motion and leaves us alone, making only an occasional dramatic appearance. It's hard to love God if that's your view of Him. But I believe the opposite is true. God is more attentive to His children than the most loving mother or caring father. Isaiah quoted God when he wrote:

> Can a mother forget the baby at her breast
> and have no compassion on the child she has borne?
> Though she may forget,
> I will not forget you!
> See, I have engraved you on the palms of My hands. . . .
> (Isaiah 49:15-16)

You and I are engraved on God's hands. He continually thinks about us and knows what is best for us. Every event and every relationship fit into His grand plan to bless us and to fulfill His purposes on earth. We don't have to be aware of all those things; we only have to be sure that He knows.

God is incredibly attentive to every detail of our lives. He dots the i's and crosses the t's and leaves nothing undone. God wants me to trust Him even for the little things in my life, which I haven't always done. Recently, I've asked the Lord to forgive me a number of times for thinking that I'm in charge of things. I'm not. He gives me responsibilities which I try to carry out to the best of my ability, but He must produce results and change lives. If He doesn't, nothing significant will happen. In the past, I've thought, *The Lord doesn' t care if I buy this hundr ed head of cattle. I'm not even going to bother Him in prayer about it.*   But the Lord has let me know: "Charlie, I am interested in everything! Bring even the details to Me, and I'll give you wisdom."

In my study of people and the Bible, I've never seen a man or a woman accomplish much without having a great relationship with God and a strong commitment to prayer. I can't think of a single exception. I've heard people tell me, "I'd like to have God to speak to me. I want to see a great sign so I'll know it's really Him." People in Jesus' day asked for the same thing, and Jesus told them the only sign they'd get was the sign of Jonah, a reference to Jesus being in the tomb for three days before His resurrection. That wasn't exactly what the people were looking for! But didn't He give them plenty of signs? He changed hearts, He gave purpose to the lost, He healed the sick, and He forgave sinners. Those signs are good enough for me! I prayed, "Lord, I'm going for broke. I'm going to seek You and let You decide what You want to do with me. I'm Yours."

God put a sense of desperation in my heart. I wasn't desperate because I was sick or broke. I was desperate because I was more aware than ever that I was empty—completely and utterly empty—without Jesus. I wanted to be filled up with Him, so that's what I asked for. What else did I have left but to seek Him with all my heart?

I love to read and pray Paul's prayers in his letters. In his letter to the Christians in Ephesus, he prayed:

> I pray that out of His glorious riches He may strengthen you with power through His Spirit in your inner being, so that Christ may dwell in your hearts though faith. And I pray that you, being rooted and established in love, may have power, together with all the saints, to grasp how wide and long and high and deep is the love of Christ, and to know this love that surpasses knowledge—that you may be filled to the measure of all the fullness of God. (Ephesians 3:16-19)

"To know this love that surpasses knowledge. . . ." Those words are a paradox, but any Christian who has experienced God's love can understand. Knowing His love, however, doesn't mean I have to be in prayer every minute of every day. It means my life is saturated with His love, so whether I'm praying or buying cows, whether I'm studying the Bible or having dinner with Laurie, whether I'm preaching at Heartland or shoveling manure, I'm confident of God's boundless love.

Yet this love has given me a tremendous desire to spend time with God in prayer. When I recommitted my life to the Lord, I determined to pray—really pray—every day. Years ago I fell away from God because I didn't read the Word and pray to stay strong. I worked all the time, in the construction business as well as for the Lord. I visited the sick, built bridges, preached sermons, paved highways, shared the gospel with the lost, and constructed buildings. I did a lot of good things, but I was too busy. This time I wasn't going to let anything crowd out my time with God. I was determined to soak up His love and wisdom and strength.

I was committed to praying fifteen minutes every day, and I struggled through that first week or so. The first morning I prayed for what seemed like an eternity. I prayed for everybody, even people in China and Afghanistan, and then I started over on those I liked the best! I looked at my watch because I thought I might have over-prayed . . . but I'd been praying for only five minutes! I thought, *Oh, my! What am I going to do for the next ten minutes?*　But I kept praying.

Then one day I looked at my watch and I had prayed twenty minutes! After another month or so, I was praying an hour. At that point, my level of spirituality changed dramatically. I became far more aware of God's presence, and my prayers were much more of a two-way conversation instead of just reciting a wish list to Him. I prayed that way for several years. No matter what was on my schedule, I prayed an hour every day. This hour was in addition to praying when I

> The first morning I prayed for what seemed like an eternity. I prayed for everybody, even people in China and Afghanistan, and then I started over on those I liked the best! I looked at my watch because I thought I might have over-prayed . . . but I'd been praying for only five minutes!

was driving in a car, in church, or at meals. This was my time in the prayer closet.

After a few years, I became disenchanted with my time of prayer. I wanted more of God, and I had a hunch He wanted more of me, too. I committed to my people that I would pray two hours a day every day. Since I made that commitment, I can't begin to tell you what has happened in me! I don't know if my prayers are doing anything for anybody else or not, but they have radically affected me. God has convinced me more fully of His goodness and His sovereignty over every detail of my life. And He has convinced me that His ways are best so I can relax and trust Him more.

My schedule is just as busy as ever. But now I realize that the busier my schedule, the more I need to pray. Martin Luther once said, "I have so much to do today that I need to spend half of it in prayer." That's the way I feel! I have meetings to negotiate a deal about milk. I have meetings about insurance, the school, dairy equipment, the Recovery Center, the Lodge, or any of a hundred other things going on. If I'm not careful, I could get completely caught up in all those things. They could consume my time and my heart. They are important, but they aren't nearly as essential as my relationship with God, and they will only succeed if God is in His rightful place on the throne in my heart.

Prayer is the mode of conversation between myself and God so He can fill me with His perspective and His compassion. Then I have the resources of wisdom and love to

CHARLIE'S THREE CHILDREN TODAY

Rodney

Linda

Carol

The Whole Family, 1997

make good decisions in my meetings and in every encounter during the day. Wisdom does not come from man; it comes from God. Our relationship with God needs to be like our circulatory system, a continual source of nourishment and strength. If we only received blood when we were desperate for it, we would remain weak and sick. Our lives would be spent in the hospital. We have the capacity to draw on the love and wisdom of God all the time, and we need to be sure we keep those arteries unblocked by busyness, apathy, and sin.

A strong relationship with God takes great effort and experience! We have to grow into it gradually. Novices are often frustrated when they don't get what they want more quickly. An oak tree grows strong and tall by undergoing many seasons and weathering many storms. Throughout history, great Christian leaders have prayed three to five hours a day, increasing their commitment to prayer as their faith grew. I'm trying to pray ten percent of my time: that's two hours and twenty-four minutes each day. I believe God has led me to seek Him in that way. Please don't misunderstand me: I don't put people down who don't have that kind of commitment to prayer. I'm not in any way saying that I'm more spiritual than somebody who prays an hour. I'm not! But this is what the Lord has called me to do. And remember, it is not simply the time spent that is important. God is not a vending machine who tosses out blessings based on the amount of time we spend in prayer. The main thing is the richness of the relationship. Time and depth, however, go hand in hand. I determined to pray for fifteen minutes, and the Lord blessed me so much that I wanted to pray for an hour. As I prayed an hour, the Lord blessed me incredibly, so I was drawn to Him for two hours each day. At every point, my relationship with God deepened, and I desired more than ever to know Him and please Him.

One of the things I battle in prayer, and I understand I am not alone in this struggle, is that my mind tends to wander. I'm praying, but I'm thinking about other things! That grieves me, but maybe God doesn't get too upset about it because He figures I'm going to get back on track pretty soon.

I am concerned about the preaching in some churches which teaches that we really don't have to do anything because it's all been done for us. Clearly, we can't earn our salvation, but we have the responsibility to respond to the grace of God by pursuing Him, obeying Him, and making choices every to live in a way that honors Him. Paul wrote about the motivation and the method of making these choices:

> Therefore, I urge you, brothers, in view of God's mercy, to offer your bodies as living sacrifices, holy and pleasing to God—this is your spiritual act of worship. Do not conform any longer to the pattern of this world, but be transformed by the renewing of your mind. Then you will be able to test and approve what God's will is—His good, pleasing, and perfect will. (Romans 12:1-2)

Heartland Christian Academy

Salvation is a free gift, a gift of grace, but the outworking of that salvation in our daily experience consists of thousands of choices to follow God's will instead of our own. We demonstrate God's presence in our lives by being generous instead of selfish, by forgiving instead of harboring bitterness, by seeking God's righteousness more than the approval of others, by trusting Him to provide instead of forcing our will on others, and by believing that He has a purpose when we encounter difficulties instead of giving up in despair.

Some believers think God has promised them a life free from difficulties. These people haven't read their Bibles! God has promised that we will experience hardships and trials, and He has promised to give us wisdom and strength to endure them. We can't have genuine strength without facing trials. Here at the farm, we plant corn in the spring. If it rains a lot when the corn is sprouting, the roots grow along the top of the soil. Later, when the dry months come, that corn withers because its roots aren't deep enough. But if some dry weeks occur early in the growth cycle, the corn sends roots down deep. Later, when the truly dry months come along, those roots can reach the hidden moisture and nourish the plant.

> Some believers think God has promised them a life free from difficulties. These people haven't read their Bibles!

We need to let adversity send our roots deep into the soil of God's love and sovereignty. Then, when we go through dry months of heartache and difficulty, those deep roots can tap into the nourishment we need. When we experience dry times, we need to realize that they are opportunities to sink our roots down deep. A lot of people want blessings without hardship, but that's not the way life is. Nothing good happens on the mountaintop—except that you can see the next mountaintop. Genuine growth takes place in the valley. I may not have learned many lessons in my life, but I have learned this one well.

Unfortunately, too many people struggle to deal with hardships that arise as a consequence of some sin. Today when something bad happens to me, I pray first, "Lord, search me. Is it me? Have I done anything to cause this problem?" I would say ninety percent of my trials are self-inflicted. The Bible teaches that the consequences of our sins can lead us to repent and change our ways. This is a mark of the grace of God to help us change!

The law of sowing and reaping applies to good and bad, to wheat and weeds:

> Do not be deceived: God cannot be mocked. A man reaps what he sows. The one who sows to please his sinful nature, from that nature will reap destruction; the one who sows to please the Spirit, from the Spirit will reap eternal life.
> (Galatians 6:7-8)

This "law of the harvest" means we will always experience the consequences of our choices, whether good or bad. We reap what we sow; we reap after we sow; and we reap more than we sow. For example, if we are bitter and hateful, people will be bitter toward us. It may take a while for their hearts to harden against us, but after gossip and hatred are ignited, we experience even more than we dished out. Conversely, if our children see in us good examples of love and consistency, they usually take on those qualities. In fact, their lives may reflect more compassion and stability than we have shown them, but such fruit may not be evident when they are toddlers or adolescents. It becomes a reality when they reach adulthood and have children of their own.

Even when we "sow the wind and reap the whirlwind," we can learn from our mistakes and grow stronger and wiser. I've learned a lot from the terrible things that have happened to me in my life. If I hadn't determined to come out of them a better man, it would all have been in vain. It is painful to reap the consequences of sin, but it is even more tragic to fail to learn from those experiences. When we encounter difficulties, our response should be: "Lord, what do You want to teach me?"

I have never understood people who say: "I was really mad at God." Personally, I have never been able to be mad at God. That attitude doesn't make any sense to me in the least. I read in the Psalms that David and the other psalmists are upset with God. They expressed their disappointment with God when they wrote things like, "How long, O Lord? Will You forget me for-

> When we encounter difficulties, our response should be: "Lord, what do You want to teach me?"

ever? How long will You hide Your face from me?" (Psalm 13:1) In most cases, however, they spent time with God and gained fresh perspective on their circumstances. Each of these psalms then ended with a sense of trust in God and hope in the future, not anger and depression. When I look at the stunts I've pulled, I'm not angry at God when I experience the consequences of them. Actually, I'm amazed that I got out as easily as I did! The consequences usually aren't as bad as I thought they might be.

One of the girls who stayed at our home commented one day, "I've never seen a Christian who really lived the Christian life." That statement bothered me a lot. I knew she had grown up going to church, but obviously she didn't have any role models who made an impact on her. I told her, "I want to tell you something: You have a right to watch me. I certainly have a long way to go to be the person the Lord wants me to be, but watch me. I want to be a good example so that someday you will say, 'I want what you've got.' Watch me, and see if you can see the love of Jesus in me. When I mess up, I'll admit it and ask for forgiveness from God and anyone else I've hurt. I won't lie to you about it, and if I've hurt anybody, I won't try to sweep it under the rug by saying, 'This is just between God and me.' "

Paul was so aware of how his behavior affected other people that he wouldn't even eat certain foods. He wanted his behavior to honor God and to be a positive example for anyone who was watching. Paul wrote to the believers in Philippi:

Carrying the message

Finally, brothers, whatever is true, whatever is noble, whatever is right, whatever is pure, whatever is lovely, whatever is admirable—if anything is excellent or praiseworthy—think about such things. Whatever you have learned or received or heard from me, or seen in me—put it into practice. And the God of peace will be with you.
(Philippians 4:8-9)

Was Paul being arrogant in telling people to watch him? No, he trusted that God would fill him, direct him, and use him as a good example. He never expected to do it in his own strength. He was 100 percent sold out to Jesus Christ, so he could be both bold and humble at the same time. Paul knew he was responsible to live in a way that showed the character of Christ to others, and he didn't shrink from that responsibility. In the same way, I also feel responsible to be an example to others. Living for Christ in obedience to Him is not merely an option for me. I am called to live a life worthy of Him, and I feel compelled to do so.

Today we sometimes hear pastors say, "Don't put your eyes on men. Keep your eyes on Jesus." If they are talking about the source of salvation, strength, and wisdom, they are right. Jesus is the only answer. But it is totally appropriate for us to look at Christian leaders and keep our eyes on them to learn how to respond to adversity, to love the unlovely, to share the gospel with the lost, to build a rich family life, and to live every moment a way that pleases the One to whom we belong. As I try to be a good example for others, I am well aware of my shortcomings, so I try to be painfully honest when I am wrong. That, too, is a part of following Christ and being a good example. If people are then drawn to Christ, if their lives are changed for the good in any way, it is a mark of the grace of God. Being a good example is a tremendous responsibility, but it is also a wonderful privilege to represent the Savior as His ambassador.

I recognized God's hand in my life throughout the good times and the bad: when Ozark flourished, and when my best friends betrayed me; when I fell in love with Laurie, and when our relationship was so painful. I prayed to God throughout these times, and He spoke to me even when I was far from Him. I never doubted that He was there and that He cared. No matter what kind of situation we are in, Christ is the answer. His grace, mercy, peace, and power cover all our sins and all our needs, and He never gives up on us.

> Being a good example is a tremendous responsibility, but it is also a wonderful privilege to represent the Savior as His ambassador.

One of the passages in the Bible that means a lot to me describes God's great mercy. Asaph was angry and grieved when he didn't understand God's plan, but even when Asaph was at his worst, God was still near and nurturing. The psalmist wrote:

> When my heart was grieved
> and my spirit embittered,
> I was senseless and ignorant;

I was a brute beast before You.
Yet I am always with You;
You hold me by my right hand.
You guide me with Your counsel,
and afterward You will take me into glory.
Whom have I in heaven but You?
And earth has nothing I desire besides You.
But as for me, it is good to be near God.
I have made the Sovereign Lord my refuge;
I will tell of all Your deeds.
(Psalm 73:21-25,28)

Even when I was at my worst, God still held my hand and led me. Even when I was sinning, God was preparing a way for me to repent and serve Him. If He had been only just, He should have disowned me for good, but He is also full of grace and mercy. As the psalmist says over and over, "His love never fails." Many times we can't see the hand of God because we aren't looking for it or because our vision is clouded by hurt or sadness. But even when we can't see God's hand, it is moving in our lives to draw us to Himself and shape a future for us.

AL
WEBER

—Executive
Vice President
and Treasurer
for Ozark Na-
tional   Life
Insurance
Company

In the early to mid 80s, I was employed by Price Waterhouse. Ozark was one of our clients, and in that relationship, I got to know Charlie Sharpe and his organization. In 1987, one of the top executives at Ozark left the company, and I was offered the position. I jumped at the chance to work for such a fine organization.

Charlie does an exceptional job of balancing the home office function of showing a profit and motivating the agency force. That is a difficult task, but it is one Charlie does very well. As an excellent speaker, Charlie encourages the agents, but he also motivates them by his integrity and honesty. He talks about being fair to people, but Charlie is always more than fair. He goes that extra step to be sure people are satisfied. It's hard to satisfy people sometimes, but Charlie really tries. That's one of the reasons people inside and outside the company appreciate him so much.

Our agents are always thankful when Charlie comes to their communities to speak at promotional dinners. Often we have over 200 people at these events. He has such high energy, and he communicates with tremendous compassion. Charlie relates to them so well that many of them want to do business with our company. Charlie is tremendously busy, so his secretary Rhonda must ensure that his schedule is as efficient as possible to get him wherever people want him—which is everywhere! Charlie is not a young man anymore, but he stays incredibly involved in the company and in our people's lives. We all appreciate that very much.

Charlie is a dream boss for me. He gives me, and everyone else who works with him, enough rope to succeed . . . or to fail. He has never had anyone to steer him back on track if he gets off, so he's had to ask himself the hard questions and come up with the answers. He's done a magnificent job of that, and I really respect his integrity and discipline. I've always tried to pattern myself after Charlie by asking myself hard questions and doing what is right no matter what.

After I had been at Ozark for only one year, the position of Executive Vice President became available. Charlie easily could have gone outside the company to fill the position, but instead he asked me if I was interested. I knew I was not ready for the position, but he worked with me and allowed me to grow into the job. I will never be able to thank him enough for the opportunity he gave me.

Charlie is very loyal to his people. He gives people a lot, and he expects a lot. In that environment, most people rise to Charlie's expectations and are more competent and successful than they ever thought possible. He provides opportunities for everyone to go beyond anything they've ever done before. That is certainly the mark of a great leader.

Many companies experience some conflict between the goals of the home office versus the goals of the field agents. Charlie creates a great balance between the two. Whenever he has to say "no" to someone, he explains his reasoning. For that reason, people don't see any decision as arbitrary and uncaring. There are very few leaders who do that for their people. He creates a very positive environment.

On a personal level, the only downside in working with Charlie is that I don't get to spend more time with him. I've learned so much from him—and I continue to learn a lot from him every time I'm with him. We are all very glad he is following his vision to develop Heartland. I only wish he could be both places at one time.

People ask me if I've seen changes in Charlie since he found the Lord a few years ago. He's the same very generous, caring, terrific leader he was before. Charlie has always been a man who has been more than fair with people, and his integrity has always been strong. But when he speaks now, he always talks very openly about the Lord. He didn't do that in my first five or six years here. The vast majority of people really appreciate his relationship with God. A few don't, but that doesn't stop him at all. A few things about his personal life have changed, and he feels motivated to set a good moral example today.

The employees at Ozark love Charlie Sharpe, especially those who have been here many years. They have not forgotten the Christmas season in which Charlie reached into his own pocket to pay Christmas bonuses to everyone because ICH Corporation chose not to do so. Charlie did not tell anyone what he had done, but the employees soon found out when the people in accounting began investigating. Word finally got around that Charlie had given the money himself. Now, that kind of loyalty to employees really makes a difference. The people who were here at that time will always remember that day.

Charlie is the same kind of man today that he was when he gave those bonuses. That's probably the biggest reason people love him, and that's why people are so loyal to him in return. Loyalty begets loyalty.

RHONDA MORGAN

—Charlie's Secretary

I started working for Ozark in 1987 as a word processor. A few months later, Charlie's secretary left the company, and they began interviewing for a replacement. At that point, Charlie and I had spoken to each other in the hall only a few times, so I was surprised when they called me to see if I was interested in becoming his secretary. To be considered, I would have to interview with Charlie, the President, and with Donald Crews, the Executive Vice President. I was a single parent, and I saw this as an opportunity to take a step to better myself.

One of the things I noticed right away when I met with Charlie was that he made me feel so comfortable. He was the President and Chairman of the Board of the company, but he instantly put me at ease. He was that way then, and he is the same way now. That is one of the things I admire about him the most.

The interviews went well, and I was offered the job. I realized immediately how incredibly busy he was! I wondered, *How can he travel as much as he does and answer so many phone calls and make so many decisions?!* I traveled to sales meetings where he spoke and watched him in action. By the time we got home, I was exhausted! I was twenty-three years old and tired, but all that work and travel and speaking didn't faze him a bit. He has incredible energy. After all these years, I've yet to find anybody anywhere as busy as Charlie.

I love working for Ozark, and I love working for Charlie. He is one of my best friends. I have learned so much from him. This is not a job to me. I get up every day and come to the office because I love doing it. I get paid for being with my friends! You can't beat that.

Charlie is the most unselfish person I have ever met. He has a lot of money, and he is the president of a company, but he never presents himself as better than anyone else. He treats everybody the same. When I interviewed to be his secretary, people asked, "Aren't you nervous? He is the company president!" But he puts people at ease by treating them as equals, so my answer to them was "no."

When I started working for Ozark, I had just gotten a divorce. I felt down. I had lost confidence in myself, but Charlie gave it back to me. He made me feel good about myself. That was a very bad time for me, but he was a real friend to encourage me and believe in me—even when I didn't believe in myself. Charlie genuinely cares for people, and they know it. He was as kind to me the first day as he is today. He is amazingly consistent.

Over the years, Charlie probably has had a lot of opportunities to sell the company and make a lot of money, but that's not what is most important to him. He wants to provide stable jobs for us. He knows we have families who count on our jobs. He is very loyal to us, and we respond by being very loyal to him. People are either loyal or they aren't. They are either dedicated to something or they aren't. Charlie talks often about making commitments that are genuine and that last through hard times, and he models that kind of commitment. Charlie is dedicated and he works hard. He expects that same commitment from others, and he rewards it when he finds it in us.

On occasions, I have been offered positions to work for other companies, but I have always turned them down because I would not think of working for anyone else. I love Charlie, and I love his company. There is never even a thought to leave here.

I enjoy watching Charlie and what is happening at Heartland. Charlie uses all he has to help people. He never puts himself first. He could retire and live in luxury, but he has gone the other direction. Many times, when people get money, they change and become more self-centered. Charlie is not that way at all. He uses his money to give generously and serve others. I have heard him say that his parents were poor but hard-working and generous. Charlie saw those qualities in them every day, and he became like them. I hope I am doing the same things for my children that Charlie's parents did for him.

EPILOGUE

From the inception of this book project, it has been my prayer and my hope that people who read it will be touched by God. All of us have needs—deep needs—which can be met only by the power of God. In John's gospel, he wrote: "For the law was given through Moses; grace and truth came through Jesus Christ." Some of us attempt to live by the law, trying to be good enough to earn God's acceptance so we can go to heaven. We work very hard, and when we fail, we hope to feel bad enough long enough to make up for our sins. But that system just doesn't work. We can never possibly do enough to earn God's acceptance, so we may as well quit trying.

Our sins separate us from God, and unless they are forgiven they result in death—separation from God for all of eternity. That's what the cross of Christ is all about. We deserve death, but the Good News is that death is the extreme price Jesus paid for us. He died in our place to pay the penalty for our sins. Under the Old Testament law, unblemished lambs were sacrificed to atone for sins. That's why Jesus was called "the Lamb of God, who takes away the sin of the world" (John 1:29). We can't possibly earn salvation because it is a free gift.

Some of us see the free gift of God's grace and forgiveness, and we gladly accept it and become His children. Some of us turn up our noses at it and insist on continuing to strive to "earn" heaven. Still others believe they are so desperately wicked that God could never love them. But the message shouted from every page of the Bible is that God, in His infinite, amazing grace, reaches out to even the most wicked and wayward sinners. He reached out to tax gatherers, Pharisees, and kings. He reached out even to me . . . and to you.

> He reached out to tax gatherers, Pharisees, and kings. He reached out even to me . . . and to you.

Some people refuse to take His hand because they are afraid they will give up too much. They fail to realize all the riches of love, strength, wisdom, and power granted freely to those who believe. Nothing on earth can possibly compare with that! We need to pry our fingers off the dirt clods of power and prestige we foolishly value so we can grasp in our hands the jewels and gold of God's grace.

My friend, have you grasped the grace of God? Do you sense the love of the Father for you? If you were to die today, are you sure you'd go to Heaven? If you haven't trusted Christ to forgive you and bring you into His family, or if you have strayed and need to recommit your life to Him, I invite you to pray this prayer:

> Lord Jesus, I need You. I am a sinner, and I need You to forgive me and make me whole. Thank You for loving me and not leaving me on my own. Come into my life as my Savior and Lord, work deep in my heart, and make me the person You want me to be. Fill me with Your Spirit, and help me to always live in a way that brings honor to You. Amen.

If you expressed that desire to God, you can be sure He answered your prayer because He is faithful. At this moment, many new things happened to you:

- All your sins have been forgiven by Christ.
- You now have eternal life.
- You became a child of God.
- Jesus has become your dearest friend.
- The power of the Holy Spirit is available to guide and strengthen you.

To grow in this wonderful relationship, take time to read the Bible regularly. I suggest you start with the Gospel of John. Pray to God. Pour out your heart to Him and trust Him with every need you have. Be sure to spend time with God's people learning more about Christ and worshiping Him in the fellowship of a local church. When you struggle with sin, repent. Turn from that sin and make choices to do what is good, right, and honoring to God.

All these things are important in nurturing your growing faith. Practice them faithfully, and you will mature in your love for God and your ability to bring Him the honor He richly deserves.

I'd like to hear from you. If you have trusted Christ as a result of reading this book, or if God has touched your heart in some way to encourage you and motivate you to live for Him, please write me a note.

Also, if you want more information about our ministry here at Heartland, please write us so we can explain how we might serve you, your family, and your friends. People from all over the country—and all over the world—are finding out about us. We welcome straying men and women who will make commitments to repent and follow Christ. We also need competent, caring, mature men and women who can help shepherd these people to grow in Christ. And of course, if you want to contribute to this ministry, we'll be happy for you to join us in that way, too.

Contact me at::

Charlie Sharpe
Heartland Ministries
400 New Creation Road North
Newark, MO 63458

phone: (660) 284-6212
e-mail address: Lsharpe@marktwain.net